JOHN CLARE

Paul Farley was born in Liverpool in 1965. He has published four collections of poetry, *The Boy from the Chemist is Here to See You*, *The Ice Age*, *Tramp in Flames* and, most recently, *The Dark Film*.

JOHN CLARE
Poems selected by PAUL FARLEY

FABER & FABER

First published in 2007
by Faber & Faber Ltd
Bloomsbury House
74–77 Great Russell Street
London WC1B 3DA

This edition published in 2016

Printed in Great Britain by
CPI Group (UK) Ltd, Croydon, CR0 4YY

A CIP record for this book
is available from the British Library

ISBN 978-0-571-32874-1

10 9 8 7 6 5 4 3 2 1

Contents

Introduction

Should you ever find yourself travelling by rail north out of London, heading to Newcastle or Edinburgh and beyond, sit on the right facing forward, and as the train begins to reach full speed in the flat country outside Peterborough you might notice a level crossing flashing by. At this point, in this blink-and-you'll-miss-it moment, you are also passing over King Street, a Roman road, and Lolham Bridges (or Brigs), a raised section designed to negotiate the River Welland's flood plain. Under one of its arches, guarded with nettles and occupied by rusty tin cans and a burned-out abandoned cooker, you would find the name 'J Clare, Helpston' scratched into the Lincolnshire limestone alongside many other lost names.

The spire at Glinton, where Clare was intermittently schooled and learned penmanship, still points into the big sky over the Fens to the east, and a day or two on foot is enough to find many of the places Clare knew so intimately in his early life. As well as scrambling down the steep weedy banks at Lolham Brigs, this could also mean stepping from a footpath into the beamy dark of Hilly Wood, pausing at the site of Langley Bush – a strange mound beneath pylons at a bend in the road – and seeking out Swordy Well behind a modern stone quarry. Sometimes, the names of places have altered slightly, as if trying to shake off the curious: so Swordy Well is now Swaddywell Pit; Royce Wood is marked as Rice Wood on the OS map of the area. But the lie of the land hasn't changed a great deal since it was enclosed two hundred years ago.

Landscape and place are so important to an understanding of Clare, because Clare ended up so 'out of it'. As a child on Emmonsales (now Ailsworth) Heath, he recalled how he'd searched for the edge of the horizon and found himself out of time: 'I eagerly wandered on and rambled among the furze the whole day till I got out of my knowledge when the very wild flowers and birds seemed to forget me and I imagined they were the inhabitants of new countries.' He finally found his way back to his village but – an echo of his contemporary Washington Irving's most famous fictional character, Rip van Winkle – everything seemed strange and altered to him.

To some degree this happens to us all, and Clare's trees and heaths and quarries and bridges, together with the micro-climate of a Northamptonshire limestone heath, stand for the landscape of childhood we all end up leaving behind and look-ing back on. We can't level the modish complaint of 'nostalgia' at Clare – time foreshortens a life lived and reflected on – but what we see instead, throughout his writing life, is somebody who has to keep returning to that first terrain. His sense of remove from it can only have been heightened by the subse-quent enclosure of Helpston and its neighbouring parishes when Clare was in his teens: fences went up, waste ground was ploughed into, old trees were uprooted, springs were sealed or diverted. The dreamtime of a childhood spent largely out of doors, keyed into a centuries-old way of life, was dismantled before his eyes.

The alienations provoked by the 1809 Enclosure Act, altering Clare's childhood spaces and places irrevocably, are only part of the story. Clare would have been steeped in the ballad traditions and folk tales and banter of his day (he describes the Bluebell Inn next to his birth home as 'the nursery for my rhymes'), and he was far from uneducated and unlettered, having read the eighteenth-century poets – Cowper, Goldsmith, Gray and Thomson – as well as discovering earlier work through anthologies and almanac magazines like Percy's *Reliques of Ancient English Poetry*; working in the fields of rural Northamptonshire, he was at the same time aswim in a print culture that by its very nature tended to take the reader beyond what was immediate and local. He felt himself moving outside of the currents of village life, experiencing a double bind still palpable today: growing literate in a class and micro-society that doesn't need or value literacy or 'bookishness'. Offered up by his publisher John Taylor as the Northamptonshire 'peasant poet' with *Poems, Descriptive of Rural Life and Scenery* in 1820, he found himself taken to market on the back of a vogue for washerwoman poets and bricklayer poets and thresher poets that had persisted in Robert Burns's afterglow (there had been Robert Bloomfield, as well as Mary Collier, Stephen Duck and Henry Jones); on his first visit to London in March of that year, he is said to have worn an ancient overcoat like armour throughout all the dinner parties and drawing rooms endured.

The book was a hit, although it seems, by the fourth edition, his sudden fame was wearing thin. In a letter to Taylor in March 1821, he wrote: 'I am again bothered with Visitors by dozens – I was once proud of being seen – but I now am always glad to hide from them – my vanity is wearied with satisfactional disappointments & it rests easy . . .' A second collection, *The Village Minstrel*, followed in the same year, and there were three further visits to London over the course of the decade, but Clare's popularity didn't outlast it. He never stopped writing – Clare was an industry, especially when he was 'in the fit' – but a third collection in 1827, *The Shepherd's Calendar*, stalled. He'd also begun to suffer bouts of depression and illness. The relationship with Taylor became strained and vexatious. Alongside his literary life, while fans and the curious beat a path to his cottage door in Helpston, Clare had a family and a working life. People – his parents, his wife and children – had long since come to depend on him. Clare's biography isn't for the fainthearted: the son of a flail-thresher whose health failed, he was unlucky in love, often skint (Robert Graves called him 'mousepoor'), and his gradual sliding out of the ken of a reading public and into the asylum is inexorable and harrowing – but we might never have heard of him at all were it not for the ambition of all concerned during those early years.

Taylor and Hessey of Fleet Street had also published John Keats, though the closest the two poets ever came to meeting was in a note Keats scribbled at the publishers' offices on the nearest paper to hand: the back of a letter from Clare. Even though this first flush of success coincided with the high-water mark of English Romanticism, Clare never sat easily among its main players. Over time, his proximity to such a cluster of bright objects might have made it that bit harder for us to see him. William Hazlitt, so brilliant on the literary figures of the day, has nothing to remark on the subject of Clare or his poetry, though Clare had something to say about him:

> He sits a silent picture of severity. If you were to watch his face for a month you would not catch a smile there. His eyes are always turned towards the ground, except when one is turned up now and then with a sneer that cuts a bad pun and a young author's maiden table-talk to atoms.

Keats and Clare knew each other's work. The former thought 'the Description too much prevailed over the Sentiment' when shown 'Solitude', while Clare seems to have found Keats' nightingale too allusive, too reliant on a vast life-support system of Classical mythology: '. . . he often described nature as she appeared to his fancies and not as he would have described her had he witnessed the things he described'. It was 'poetical', according to Coleridge, to listen to the nightingale sing 'Philomela's pity-pleading strains' in a great thicket of resonances; but the bird Clare went on to describe in *The Rural Muse* in 1835 is the shy, skulking, dowdy creature it ever has been to anyone who's really looked for it, his poem leading us deeper into description of bird, habitat, nest, eggs:

Deep adown

The nest is made, a hermit's mossy cell.
Snug lie her curious eggs in number five
Of deadened green or rather olive-brown,
And the old prickly thorn-bush guards them well.

You have to admire the species count in Clare's poetry, too. While the Romantics tended to write about the same stock nightingales and larks, Clare is positively bio-diverse. You'd need to go back to Michael Drayton in the early seventeenth-century to find so many *kinds* of birds (Drayton also liked to assign the power of speech to an actual place). Clare's poems about birds and their nests are like nothing else, and are among his greatest gifts to English poetry. Reading them, we move closer to the centre of a universe, parallel and at the same time part of our own. Narrative detail and observation build the poems up, pentameter by pentameter, with no stanzaic separation, until we find ourselves orbiting and connected again to a secret in the world that is precious, even erotic:

> And in the old hedge bottom rot away
> Built like an oven with a little hole
> Hard to discover – that snug entrance wins
> Scarcely admitting e'en two fingers in
> And lined with feathers warm as silken stole . . .

In 'The Yellowhammer's Nest' we creep up on a clutch of eggs whose shells are described as 'pen-scribbled o'er with ink'; an early poem, 'Schoolboys in Winter', has the schoolboys looking up at wild geese moving across the sky 'watching the letters which their journeys make'. Clare really notices things – the squeak and clap of a favourite gate, the 'guggles and groans' of a brook – but at certain moments in his work, it's as if he's trying to synthesize the very act and habits of reading and writing with what's being described; as if he's pointing to how his bookishness has materially altered the way in which he sees the world. He could also write in a way that pointed towards the limits of spoken and written language, as if speech and words were inadequate (though language is sometimes a consolation): in this way we can see another double bind manifest in his poems, another way in which Clare is neither firmly here nor there but at some place in-between:

> And whether it be hill or moor,
> I feel where'er I go
> A silence that discourses more
> Than any tongue can do . . .
>   ('Pastoral Poesy')

O words are poor receipts for what time hath stole away . . .
  ('Remembrances')

Yet there by pleasure unforsook
In nature's happy moods
The cuts in Fenning's Spelling Book
Made up for fields and woods.
    ('Childhood')

The way Clare returned to the sonnet form throughout his writing life is a thing to behold. An early poem like 'The River Gwash' – Clare first saw his wife-to-be Patty while walking in the water meadows by this river – can be thought of as conventional: we can see there's a recognizable rhyme scheme, a sense of octave and sextet (though the 'turn' comes a little late) and a closing couplet. (We could pause at his 'romantic bend' and compare this with another river sonnet published the same year, Wordsworth's 'After Thought' on the Duddon: is Clare's 'While glides the stream a silver streak between' producing an impressively early echo of 'Still glides the stream and shall forever glide'?) Over time, though, all kinds of structures are explored, some of which, as Jonathan Bate has pointed out, are entirely novel and unprecedented. In a sonnet like 'Emmonsails Heath in Winter' you can see how something different is happening:

I love to see the old heath's withered brake
Mingle its crimpled leaves with furze and ling
While the old heron from the lonely lake
Starts slow and flaps his melancholy wing
And oddling crow in idle motions swing
On the half-rotten ash tree's topmost twig
Beside whose trunk the gypsy makes his bed –
Up flies the bouncing woodcock from the brig
Where a black quagmire quakes beneath the tread;
The fieldfare chatters in the whistling thorn
And for the 'awe round fields and closen rove,

And coy bumbarrels twenty in a drove
Flit down the hedgerows in the frozen plain
And hang on little twigs and start again.

As well as the admixture of rhymes – quatrain shapes and couplets, and a thorn line ending in 'thorn'! – we get what Seamus Heaney has called the 'one-thing-after-anotherness' effect a Clare poem can often generate: everything is being accorded an equal weight, and we gain a sense of circulation as opposed to progression or closure. It's as if we are reading a small strip cut out from a vast sequence of code. The first person pronoun that leads us into the poem is soon discarded and forgotten (Clare often excelled at getting himself out of the way) and the world comes close to speaking for itself. And look at the vocabulary: 'crimpled', 'oddling', 'brig', ''awe', 'bumbarrels'. Clare was an adventurous reader, well capable of literary allusion, but he never turned his back on what was regarded as provincial and vulgar ('I am of that class,' he wrote). In staying close to home, he has left us a trove of dialect words, though these non-standard nouns and adjectives and phrasings also produce all manner of sound effects, and manage to coexist in the dynamic spaces of the poems with the Latinate and the more conventional constructions familiar to the poetry of his age. Everything is moving; hierarchies and linguistic orders of succession are not put up with.

Clare's unorthodoxy meant a complex and sometimes strained relationship with his publisher that is still being played out to this day. Because his manuscripts are mostly unpunctuated, and because he used so many words from his Northamptonshire vernacular and variant spellings, the degree of Taylor's input and intervention went beyond simply correcting a few solecisms or suggesting the odd cut. On the one hand, Taylor can be viewed as 'tampering' with Clare's effusions, tidying up and toning down the poet's original intentions, but there's plenty of evidence to support the view that Clare was more than willing to be carefully edited, especially early on. He does seem to have had a robust enough attitude to his own work – any poet who could talk in terms of 'the whole of my rubbish which I have scribbled lately' doesn't seem particularly precious – together with an awareness of the marketplace, and what publishers are for. Like Keats, he wanted in. He wanted to be read, and widely. And for a time, in the early 1820s, he was.

While not wanting to tidy up and tone down, and keen to preserve Clare's dialect, I have erred on the side of light punctuation for this present selection, which is intended both as a gathering of the poems I cherish most, but also as a point of entry for those perhaps unfamiliar with his work. I got to know Clare's poems in the versions edited by Geoffrey Summerfield, published in 1990, and so tend towards dropping the ampersand, applying possessive apostrophes, and so on; more recently, Jonathan Bate has produced a *Selected Poems* (this volume draws heavily on Bate's edition, and I am grateful for his kind permission to have done so) that extends this by careful use of commas and full stops, taking the view that punctuation – while it risks harming the fluidity of Clare's verse – is a useful guide for the new reader, and can be dispensed with once familiarity has been gained. Over time, the twin poles of editorial attention – standardization and normalization at one extreme, absolute fidelity to the original manuscript at the other – can give the impression of poems that are still 'live' and unsettled. The best way to illustrate this is to simply look at the afterlife a single work has led:

The Sand-Martin

Thou hermit, haunter of the lonely glen
    And common wild and heath – the desolate face
Of rude, waste landscapes far away from men,
    Where frequent quarries give thee dwelling-place,
With strangest taste and labour undeterred
    Drilling small holes along the quarry's side,
More like the haunt of vermin than a bird,
    And seldom by the nesting boy descried –

I've seen thee far away from all thy tribe,
   Flirting about the unfrequented sky,
And felt a feeling that I can't describe
   Of lone seclusion, and a hermit joy
To see thee circle round nor go beyond
That lone heath and its melancholy pond.
       (from *The Poems of John Clare*, 1935)

Sand Martin

Thou hermit haunter of the lonely glen
& common wild & heath – the desolate face
Of rude waste landscapes far away from men
Where frequent quarrys give thee dwelling place
With strangest taste & labour undeterred
Drilling small holes along the quarrys side
More like the haunts of vermin than a bird
& seldom by the nesting boy descried
Ive seen thee far away from all thy tribe
Flirting about the unfrequented sky
& felt a feeling that I can t describe
Of lone seclusion & a hermit joy
To see thee circle round nor go beyond
That lone heath & its melancholly pond
       (from *The Midsummer Cushion*, 1979)

Sand Martin

Thou hermit haunter of the lonely glen
And common wild and heath – the desolate face
Of rude waste landscapes far away from men
Where frequent quarrys give thee dwelling place
With strangest taste and labour undeterred
Drilling small holes along the quarry's side
More like the haunts of vermin than a bird
And seldom by the nesting boy descried
I've seen thee far away from all thy tribe

Flirting about the unfrequented sky
And felt a feeling that I can't describe
Of lone seclusion and a hermit joy
To see thee circle round nor go beyond
That lone heath and its melancholly pond
(from *Selected Poetry*, 1990)

The Sand Martin

Thou hermit haunter of the lonely glen
And common wild and heath – the desolate face
Of rude waste landscapes far away from men
Where frequent quarries give thee dwelling place,
With strangest taste and labour undeterred
Drilling small holes along the quarry's side,
More like the haunts of vermin than a bird
And seldom by the nesting boy descried –
I've seen thee far away from all thy tribe
Flirting about the unfrequented sky
And felt a feeling that I can't describe
Of lone seclusion and a hermit joy
To see thee circle round nor go beyond
That lone heath and its melancholy pond.
(from *Selected Poems*, 2003)

The wakeful reader should be alerted to this state of affairs, and I'd urge anybody who enjoys the poems collected here to explore further, not only because the 'raw' poetry, transcribed faithfully from manuscript, is published and available, but also because of the sheer amount of writing I couldn't include. I was especially regretful not to have found a space for Clare's essays and prose fragments, and longer works such as *The Parish*, 'Don Juan' and 'Child Harold'.

The Romantic poets must surely have helped get Clare going – and not only in terms of the interest and mercantile space they created for poetry – just as surely as his reading of the eighteenth-century poets provided a model both to work within and against. But Clare's poetry grew in other, different directions from Romanticism. He speaks out of, and for, the fragility of the natural world and the rootedness of places – sometimes literally, the *genius loci*, as in 'The Lamentations of Round-Oak Waters' or 'The Lament of Swordy Well' – bearing witness or giving voice to a landscape being altered irrevocably, often for profit or gain, so that the very co-ordinates of our creaturely attachments to it are rendered as in disintegration. Where a poet like Wordsworth could posit a continuum, an immortality, Clare's hacked-back Langley Bush, or the fallen elm that stood next to the cottage of his birth, angrily represent a point of no return, a loss that blights self and community because a great web of interconnectedness has been snicked at and jeopardized:

> Old favourite tree, thou'st seen times changes lower,
> Though change till now did never injure thee,
> For time beheld thee as her sacred dower
> And nature claimed thee her domestic tree;
> Storms came and shook thee many a weary hour,
> Yet steadfast to thy home thy roots have been;
> Summers of thirst parched round thy homely bower
> Till earth grew iron – still thy leaves was green.

In April 1832 Clare and his family moved to a house in a Fen village, Northborough. Everybody thought this was for the best. His new home was more spacious and better appointed, but even though it lay at a short distance from Helpston – a minute or two out of a train window today – it may as well have been the other side of the world. He was now at one further remove from his 'significant earth'. His depression-like illness worsened. A curtailed version of his book *The Midsummer Cushion* was published in 1835 as *The Rural Muse*, and it was to be his last book: *The Midsummer Cushion* finally saw the light of day in 1979. While at Northborough he continued to write, but by 1837 his illness had reached a crisis point; his wife was struggling to cope with his behaviour, and Taylor, with the help of Clare's doctors, arranged to have him enter an asylum. He spent four years at High Beach in Epping Forest, before one day deciding to walk the eighty-odd miles back to Northborough (his famous prose account of this journey, eating grass and sleeping aligned to the pole star, was written soon after his arrival). His wife took him back in, but before the end of the year he was certified insane for a second time, and moved to Northampton General Lunatic Asylum. He died there in 1864.

Although some critics have complained of a narrow range to Clare's work – and this goes all the way back to John Taylor – there now seem to be several 'John Clare's. It was a long writing life, and so much of the work has survived in manuscript. He is well known now as a lyrical writer on childhood and landscape and the natural world, but he was also capable of mordant political satire (*The Parish*), of coarse and bawdy ventriloquism ('Don Juan') and downright polyphony ('Child Harold'). He wrote verse-tales, a number of arresting prose sketches and essays, an autobiography, kept a journal off and on, and was seriously considering a natural history along the lines of Gilbert White. He transcribed folk songs and dance tunes. Organizing his work in anything other than a chronological sequence might yield the bird poems of John Clare, the love poems of John Clare, or a book based entirely around his attentiveness to seasons (as he himself most obviously did in *The Shepherd's Calendar*) or the weather (beautifully attuned to exposure and shelter: poems like 'The Hail Storm in June 1831' or 'Sudden Shower' capture the detail and surprise of a change in the elements like a woodblock print by Hiroshige), or even the times of day: the latter could produce a decent sequence moving from aubade to lullaby. His life itself has tended to fall into recognizable constituent periods: Clare the 'peasant poet', 'poor Clare', the poet shut up in the madhouse and forgotten, with the flight home from Essex somewhere in the middle. Even the psycho-geographers of our time have attempted to approach and map Clare's places. Perhaps, following his relative invisibility during the Victorian era, each generation has tended to amplify one aspect of his writing, one version of John Clare.

The Irish poets who came to prominence in the 1960s led me to him: Michael Longley and Derek Mahon pointed the way, with poems in each of their first collections acting like finder stars, picking out a whole new constellation. Then there was the brilliant prose advocacy of Seamus Heaney and Tom Paulin. But behind all of them perhaps is the figure of Patrick Kavanagh: 'I found the poems in the fields/ And only wrote them down' finds an echo in Kavanagh's 'On Reading a Book on Common Wild Flowers' a century later: 'I knew them all by eye-sight long before I knew their names./ We were in love before we were introduced.' Discovering Clare through other poets is entirely in keeping with his long process of rehabilitation, a lineage of poet supporters stretching from Arthur Symons to Edward Thomas to Edmund Blunden to Geoffrey Grigson. There have also been huge feats of scholarship and biography. He is no longer a 'blink-and-you'll-miss-him' poet, poorly represented in the anthologies. Marketing and fashion, and all the other anxious freight of any age, will burn off over time, leaving us with the poems to consider, and there has been a freshness about Clare, a great sense of rediscovery, over the past forty or so years.

There must be many other reasons why Clare's popularity grows, why more and more of us are reading his poems, and one must be the question of space. Poets are often praised for their singular 'voice', when in fact what we're admiring is their slant to the world, how they set themselves, in language, in relation to it. Clare's early life coincided with the greatest spatial upheaval that the English countryside – and townscape – had seen in a millennium. Helpston's enclosure, doing away with an open field system which, crucially, Clare knew and experienced intimately, was part of a widespread break with the way people related to their world, the cyclical arrangement of its fields and the disposal of its common land. This can resonate with readers now in several ways. Our sense of the local and the quiddity of solid things in it has been adjusted by a century of cinema and television, by the ubiquity of the mechanical recording and photographed image, and more recently the explosion in telecommunications that has fundamentally altered (some might say wounded) that relationship: the process was already under way in Clare's time as print disseminated, making us, in John Barrell's phrase, 'all tourists now'. And, beyond the context of the developed West, we should also remember that huge swathes of the planet are right now on the move and undergoing their own great leaps: in China, for example, the 'face to the earth, back to the sky' way of subsistence farming is being eroded, as people migrate to the cities in great numbers. However we regard these shifts, it's entirely possible that Clare, the great poet of dwelling and displacement, has something important to say to our own times.

There is a poem called 'The Flood', written before the moves to Northborough and the asylums beyond, but turbulent and troubled and deeply disturbed on home ground near Helpston. Clare is at 'Lolham Brigs in wild and lonely mood', as we know he often liked to watch the river from this vantage point (he'd already written of it in 'The Last of March': and the annual floods at Lolham Brigs were one of the sights he said he would miss and return to see again once he'd moved away). In this poem, the river in spate has broached its banks and can actually be felt through the old stone of the bridge: 'Crash came the ice against the jambs and then/ A shudder jarred the arches'. The unpunctuated five beat line here is assailed by the dash, as clauses are ripped from their syntactical seating, and lines left hanging: 'Trays – uptorn bushes – fence demolished rails'. The world has become a 'huzzing sea', and Clare feels the chill air round him 'ocean blea': it's a vision of total elemental flux, of frightening effacement and rate of change, and the fixity of the bridge isn't tidily affirmed or asserted. Instead, the poem's end – 'On roars the flood' – is exhilarating and scary, the more so when we remember the identity of the figure on that bridge and the uncertain future he was staring into.

PAUL FARLEY

JOHN CLARE

Schoolboys in Winter

The schoolboys still their morning rambles take
To neighbouring village school with playing speed,
Loitering with pastimes' leisure till they quake,
Oft looking up the wild geese droves to heed,
Watching the letters which their journeys make,
Or plucking 'awes on which the fieldfares feed,
And hips and sloes – and on each shallow lake
Making glib slides where they like shadows go
Till some fresh pastimes in their minds awake
And off they start anew and hasty blow
Their numbed and clumpsing fingers till they glow,
Then races with their shadows wildly run
That stride, huge giants, o'er the shining snow
In the pale splendour of the winter sun.

A Ramble

How sweet and dear
To Taste's warm bosom and to health's flushed cheek
Morn's flushing face peeps out her first fond smile,
Crimsoning the east in many-tinted hue
The horizon round, as edged with brooding mist,
Penc'ling its seeming circle round so uniform
In tinge of faintly blue – how lovely then
The streak which matchless nature, skirting sweet,
Flushes the edges of the arching sky
And melting draws the hangings of the morn.
O who that lives as free to mark the charms
Of nature's earliest dress, far from the smoke
And cheerless bustle of the city's strife,
To breathe the cool sweet air, mark the blue sky
And all the nameless beauties limning morn
So beautifully touches, who when free
By drowsy slumbers e'er would be detained,
Snoring supinely o'er their idle dreams,
Would lie to lose a charm so charming now
As is the early morn – come now, we'll start,
Arise my dog and shake thy curdled coat
And bark thy friendly symptoms by my side,
Tracing the dewy plains we'll muse along.
Behind us left our nookèd track wild wound
From bush to bush as rambling on we tread,
Peeping on dew-gilt branch, moist grassy tuft
And nature's every trifle e'er so mean –
Her every trifle pleases much mine eye –
So on we hie to witness what she wears:
How beautiful e'en seems
This simple twig that steals it from the hedge
And wavering dipples down to taste the stream.
I cannot think it how the reason is

That every trifle nature's bosom wears
Should seem so lovely and appear so sweet
And charm so much my soul while heedless passenger
Soodles me by, an animated post,
And ne'er so much as turns his head to look
But stalks along as though his eyes were blinded
And as if the witching face of nature
Held but now a dark unmeaning blank.
  O Taste, thou charm
That so endears and nature makes so lovely,
Nameless enthusiastic ardour thine,
That'wildered 'witching rapture 'quisitive,
Stooping bent, genius o'er each object – thine
That longing pausing wishing that cannot pass
Uncomprehended things without a sigh
For wisdom to unseal the hidden cause –
That 'ankering gaze is thine that fainly would
Turn the blue blinders of the heavens aside
To see what gods are doing.

The Lamentations of Round-Oak Waters

Oppress'd wi' grief a double share
  Where Round Oak Waters flow,
I one day took a sitting there
  Recounting many a woe.
My naked seat without a shade
  Did cold and blealy shine,
Which fate was more agreeable made
  As sympathising mine.

The wind between the north and east
  Blow'd very chill and cold
Or coldly blow'd to me at least:
  My clothes were thin and old.
The grass all dropping wet wi' dew
  Low bent their tiny spears;
The lowly daisy bended too
  More lowly wi' my tears.

(For when my wretched state appears
  Hurt, friendless, poor and starv'd,
I never can withold my tears
  To think how I am sarv'd;
To think how money'd men delight
  More cutting than the storm,
To make a sport and prove their might
  O'er me a fellow worm.)

With arms reclin'd upon my knee
  In melancholy form,
I bow'd my head to misery
  And yielded to the storm.
And there I fancied uncontrolled;
  My sorrows, as they flew

Unnotic'd as the waters rolled,
　　Were all unnoticed too.

But soon I found I was deceiv'd
　　For, waken'd by my woes,
The naked stream, of shade bereav'd,
　　In grievous murmurs rose:

'Ah luckless youth to sorrow born,
　　Shun'd son of Poverty,
The world's made gamely sport and scorn
　　And grinning infamy;
Unequall'd tho thy sorrows seem –
　　And great indeed they are –
O hear my sorrows for my stream:
　　You'll find an equal there.

'I am the genius of the brook
　　And like to thee I moan,
By naiads and by all forsook,
　　Unheeded and alone.
Distress and sorrow quickly proves
　　The friend sincere and true;
Soon as our happiness removes
　　Pretenders bid adieu.

'Here I have been for many a year,
　　And how my brook has been,
How pleasures lately flourish'd here
　　Thy self has often seen.
The willows waving wi' the wind
　　And here and there a thorn
Did please thy melancholy mind
　　And did my banks adorn.

'And here the shepherd with his sheep
　　And with his lovely maid
Together where these waters creep
　　In loitering dalliance play'd;

And here the cowboy lov'd to sit
    And plait his rushy thongs
And dabble in the fancied pit
    And chase the minnow throngs.

'And when thou didst thy horses tend
    Or drive the ploughman's team,
Thy mind did naturally bend
    Towards my pleasing stream,
And different pleasures fill'd thy breast
    And different thy employ
And different feelings thou possessed
    From any other boy.

'The sports which they so dearly lov'd
    Thou couldst not bear to see,
And joys which they as joys approv'd
    Ne'er seem'd as joys to thee;
The joy was thine couldst thou but steal
    From all their gambols rude
In some lone thicket to conceal
    Thyself in solitude.

'There didst thou joy and love to sit
    The briars and brakes among,
To exercise thy infant wit
    In fancied tale or song;
And there the insect and the flower
    Would court thy curious eye
To muse in wonder on that power
    Which dwells above the sky.

'But now alas my charms are done
    For shepherds and for thee;
The cowboy with his green is gone
    And every bush and tree.
Dire nakedness o'er all prevails;
    Yon fallows bare and brown

Is all beset wi' posts and rails
　　And turned upside down.

'The gently curving darksome bawks
　　That stript the cornfields o'er
And prov'd the shepherd's daily walks
　　Now prove his walks no more;
The plough has had them under hand
　　And over turnd 'em all
And now along the elting land
　　Poor swains are forc'd to maul

'And where yon furlong meets the lawn
　　To ploughmen Oh! how sweet
When they had their long furrow drawn
　　Its eddings to their feet,
To rest 'em while they clean their plough
　　And light their loaded shoe,
But ah – there's ne'er an edding now
　　For neither them nor you.

'The bawks and eddings are no more,
　　The pastures too are gone,
The greens, the meadows and the moors
　　Are all cut up and done;
There's scarce a greensward spot remains
　　And scarce a single tree;
All naked are thy native plains
　　And yet they're dear to thee.

'But O! my brook, my injur'd brook,
　　'Tis that I most deplore
To think how once it us'd to look
　　How it must look no more.
And hap'ly fate thy wanderings bent
　　To sorrow here wi' me,
For to none else could I lament
　　And mourn to none but thee.

'Thou art the whole of musing swains
     That's now residing here,
Tho one ere while did grace my plains
     And he to thee was dear.
Ah – dear he was – for now I see
     His name grieves thee at heart:
Thy silence speaks that Misery
     Which language can't impart.

'O T—l T—l dear should thou
     To this fond Mourner be
By being so much troubl'd now
     From just a nameing thee;
Nay I as well as he am griev'd
     For oh I hop'd of thee
That hadst thou stay'd as I believ'd
     Thou wouldst have griev'd for me.

'But ah he's gone, the first o' swains,
     And left us both to moan,
And thou art all that now remains
     With feelings like his own.
So while the thoughtless passes by
     Of sense and feelings void,
Thine be the fancy painting eye
     On bygone scenes employ'd.

'Look backward on the days of yore
     Upon my injur'd brook;
In fancy con its beauties o'er,
     How it had us'd to look.
O then what trees my banks did crown,
     What willows flourishd here:
Hard as the axe that cut them down
     The senseless wretches were.

'But sweating slaves I do not blame,
  Those slaves by wealth decreed;
No: I should hurt their harmless name
  To brand 'em wi' the deed.
Although their aching hands did wield
  The axe that gave the blow,
Yet 't'was not them that own'd the field
  Nor plan'd its overthrow.

'No, no: the foes that hurt my field
  Hurt these poor moilers too,
And thy own bosom knows and feels
  Enough to prove it true.
And o poor souls they may complain
  But their complainings all
The injur'd worms that turn again
  But turn again to fall.

'Their foes and mine are lawless foes
  And laws themselves they hold
Which clipt-wing'd justice cant oppose
  But, forced, yields to gold.
These are the foes of mine and me;
  These all our ruin plan'd
Although they never felld a tree
  Or took a tool in hand.

'Ah cruel foes, with plenty blest,
  So hankering after more
To lay the greens and pastures waste
  Which profited before.
Poor greedy souls – what would they have
  Beyond their plenty given?
Will riches keep 'em from the grave?
  Or buy them rest in heaven?'

What is Life?

And what is life? An hourglass on the run,
A mist retreating from the morning sun,
A busy bustling still repeated dream.
Its length? A minute's pause, a moment's thought.
And happiness? A bubble on the stream
That in the act of seizing shrinks to nought.

What are vain hopes? The puffing gale of morn
That of its charms divests the dewy lawn
And robs each flow'ret of its gem – and dies;
A cobweb hiding disappointment's thorn,
Which stings more keenly through the thin disguise.

And thou, O trouble? Nothing can suppose
(And sure the power of wisdom only knows)
What need requireth thee:
So free and liberal as thy bounty flows,
Some necessary cause must surely be.
But disappointments, pains and every woe
Devoted wretches feel,
The universal plagues of life below,
Are mysteries still 'neath fate's unbroken seal.

And what is death? Is still the cause unfound?
That dark mysterious name of horrid sound?
A long and lingering sleep the weary crave.
And peace? Where can its happiness abound?
Nowhere at all save heaven and the grave.

Then what is life? When stripped of its disguise,
A thing to be desired it cannot be,
Since everything that meets our foolish eyes
Gives proof sufficient of its vanity –

'Tis but a trial all must undergo,
To teach unthankful mortals how to prize
That happiness vain man's denied to know
Until he's called to claim it in the skies.

The Gypsies' Evening Blaze

To me how wildly pleasing is that scene
Which doth present in evening's dusky hour
A group of gypsies centred on the green
In some warm nook where Boreas has no power,
Where sudden starts the quivering blaze behind
Short shrubby bushes nibbled by the sheep
That mostly on these shortsward pastures keep,
Now lost, now seen, now bending with the wind:
And now the swarthy sybil kneels reclined,
With proggling stick she still renews the blaze,
Forcing bright sparks to twinkle from the flaze.
When this I view, the all-attentive mind
Will oft exclaim (so strong the scene pervades)
'Grant me this life, thou spirit of the shades!'

The River Gwash

Where winding Gwash whirls round its wildest scene,
On this romantic bend I sit me down;
On that side view the meadow's smoothing green
Edged with the peeping hamlet's chequering brown,
Here the steep bank, as dropping headlong down,
While glides the stream a silver streak between,
As glide the shaded clouds along the sky,
Bright'ning and deep'ning, losing as they're seen,
In light and shade, to where old willows lean;
Thus their broad shadow runs the river by,
With tree and bush replete, a' wildered scene,
And moss and ivy speckling on my eye.
O thus while musing wild, I'm doubly blest,
My woes unheeding and my heart at rest.

Song

Swamps of wild rush-beds and sloughs' squashy traces,
  Grounds of rough fallows with thistle and weed,
Flats and low valleys of kingcups and daisies,
  Sweetest of subjects are ye for my reed:
Ye commons left free in the rude rags of nature,
  Ye brown heaths beclothed in furze as ye be,
My wild eye in rapture adores every feature,
  Ye are dear as this heart in my bosom to me.

O native endearments, I would not forsake ye,
  I would not forsake ye for sweetest of scenes;
For sweetest of gardens that nature could make me,
  I would not forsake ye, dear valleys and greens:
Though nature ne'er dropt ye a cloud-resting mountain,
  Nor waterfalls tumble their music so free;
Had nature denied ye a bush, tree, or fountain,
  Ye still had been loved as an Eden by me.

And long, my dear valleys, long, long may ye flourish,
  Though rush-beds and thistles make most of your pride;
May showers never fail the green's daisies to nourish,
  Nor suns dry the fountain that rills by its side.
Your skies may be gloomy and misty your mornings,
  Your flat swampy valleys unwholesome may be;
Still, refuse of nature, without her adornings
  Ye are dear as this heart in my bosom to me.

To an Infant Daughter

Sweet gem of infant fairy-flowers,
Thy smiles on life's unclosing hours
Like sunbeams lost in summer showers,
  They wake my fears;
When reason knows its sweets and sours,
  They'll change to tears.

God help thee, little senseless thing,
Thou, daisy-like of early spring,
Of ambushed winter's hornet sting
  Hast yet to tell;
Thou know'st not what tomorrows bring:
  I wish thee well.

But thou art come, and soon or late
'Tis thine to meet the frowns of fate,
The harpy grin of envy's hate,
  And mermaid-smiles
Of worldly folly's luring bait,
  That youth beguiles.

And much I wish, what'er may be
The lot, my child, that falls to thee,
  Her glass betimes,
But keep thee from my failings free –
  Nor itch at rhymes.

Lord help thee in thy coming years
If thy mad father's picture 'pears
Predominant – his feeling fears
  And jingling starts;
I'd freely now gi'vent to tears
  To ease my heart.

May thou, unknown to rhyming bother,
Be ignorant as is thy mother,
And in thy manners such another,
        Save sin's nigh guest;
And then wi' 'scaping this and t'other
        Thou mayst be blest.

Lord knows my heart, it loves thee much;
And may my feelings, aches and such,
The pains I meet in folly's clutch
        Be never thine:
Child, it's a tender string to touch,
        That sounds 'Thou'rt mine.'

Langley Bush

O Langley Bush, the shepherd's sacred shade,
   Thy hollow trunk oft gained a look from me;
Full many a journey o'er the heath I've made,
   For such-like curious things I love to see.
What truth the story of the swain allows,
   That tells of honours which thy young days knew,
Of 'Langley Court' being kept beneath thy boughs,
   I cannot tell – thus much I know is true,
That thou art reverenced: even the rude clan
   Of lawless gypsies, driven from stage to stage,
Pilfering the hedges of the husbandman,
   Spare thee, as sacred, in thy withering age.
Both swains and gypsies seem to love thy name,
   Thy spot's a favourite with the sooty crew,
And soon thou must depend on gypsy-fame,
   Thy mouldering trunk is nearly rotten through.
My last doubts murmur on the zephyr's swell,
   My last look lingers on thy boughs with pain;
To thy declining age I bid farewell,
   Like old companions, ne'er to meet again.

To my Cottage

Thou lowly cot where first my breath I drew,
Past joys endear thee, childhood's past delight
Where each young summer's pictured on my view,
And, dearer still, the happy winter-night
When the storm pelted down with all his might
And roared and bellowed in the chimney-top
And pattered vehement 'gainst the window-light
And on the threshold fell the quick eaves-drop.
How blest I've listened on my corner stool,
Heard the storm rage, and hugged my happy spot,
While the fond parent wound her whirring spool
And spared a sigh for the poor wanderer's lot.
In thee, sweet hut, this happiness was proved,
And these endear and make thee doubly loved.

In Hilly Wood

How sweet to be thus nestling deep in boughs
Upon an ashen stoven pillowing me;
Faintly are heard the ploughmen at their ploughs,
But not an eye can find its way to see.
The sunbeams scarce molest me with a smile,
So thick the leafy armies gather round;
And where they do, the breeze blows cool the while,
Their leafy shadows dancing on the ground.
Full many a flower, too, wishing to be seen,
Perks up its head the hiding grass between –
In mid-wood silence, thus, how sweet to be,
Where all the noises that on peace intrude
Come from the chittering cricket, bird and bee,
Whose songs have charms to sweeten solitude.

from The Shepherd's Calendar

from MARCH

March, month of 'many weathers', wildly comes
In hail and snow and rain and threatening hums
And floods – while often at his cottage door
The shepherd stands to hear the distant roar
Loosed from the rushing mills and river-locks
With thundering sound and overpowering shocks.
From bank to bank along the meadow lea
The river spreads and shines a little sea,
While in the pale sunlight a watery brood
Of swopping white birds flock about the flood.

[. . .]

The shepherd-boy, that hastens now and then
From hail and snow beneath his sheltering den
Of flags or file-leaved sedges tied in sheaves
Or stubble shocks, oft as his eye perceives
Sun-threads shrink out in momentary smiles,
With fancy thoughts his loneliness beguiles,
Thinking the struggling winter hourly by,
As down the edges of the distant sky
The hailstorm sweeps – and while he stops to strip
The stooping hedge-briar of its lingering hip,
He hears the wild geese gabble o'er his head,
Then, pleased with fancies in his musings bred,
He marks the figured forms in which they fly
And pausing, follows with a wondering eye,
Likening their curious march in curves or rows
To every letter which his memory knows,
While, far above, the solitary crane
Swings lonely to unfrozen dykes again,

Cranking a jarring melancholy cry
Through the wild journey of the cheerless sky.

[. . .]

The insect world, now sunbeams higher climb,
Oft dream of spring and wake before their time,
Blue flies from straw stacks crawling scarce alive
And bees peep out on slabs before the hive,
Stroking their little legs across their wings
And venturing short flights where the snowdrop hings
Its silver bell – and winter aconite
With buttercup-like flowers that shut at night
And green leaf frilling round their cups of gold
Like tender maiden muffled from the cold:
They sip and find their honey dreams are vain
And feebly hasten to their hives again
And butterflies, by eager hopes undone,
Glad as a child come out to greet the sun
Lost neath the shadow of a sudden shower
Nor left to see tomorrow's April flower.

from MAY

The driving boy beside his team
Of May-month beauty now will dream
And cock his hat and turn his eye
On flower and tree and deepening sky,
And oft burst loud in fits of song
And whistle as he reels along,
Cracking his whip in starts of joy –
A happy, dirty, driving boy.
The youth who leaves his corner stool
Betimes for neighbouring village-school,
Where as a mark to guide him right
The church spire's all the way in sight,
With cheerings from his parents given,

Starts 'neath the joyous smiles of heaven
And sawns with many an idle stand,
With book-bag swinging in his hand,
And gazes as he passes by
On every thing that meets his eye.
Young lambs seem tempting him to play,
Dancing and bleating in his way –
With trembling tails and pointed ears
They follow him and lose their fears;
He smiles upon their sunny faces
And fain would join their happy races.
The birds that sing on bush and tree
Seem chirping for his company;
And all – in fancy's idle whim –
Seem keeping holiday, but him.
He lolls upon each resting stile
To see the fields so sweetly smile,
To see the wheat grow green and long,
And lists the weeder's toiling song
Or short note of the changing thrush
Above him in the whitethorn bush
That o'er the leaning stile bends low
Loaded with mockery of snow.

from JUNE

Now summer is in flower and nature's hum
Is never silent round her sultry bloom.
Insects as small as dust are never done
With glittering dance and reeling in the sun
And green wood fly and blossom-haunting bee
Are never weary of their melody.
Round field hedge now, flowers in full glory twine:
Large bindweed bells, wild hop and streaked woodbine
That lift athirst their slender-throated flowers
Agape for dewfalls and for honey showers;

These round each bush in sweet disorder run
And spread their wild hues to the sultry sun,
Where its silk netting lace on twigs and leaves
The mottled spider at eve's leisure weaves,
That every morning meet the poet's eye
Like fairies' dew-wet dresses hung to dry.
The wheat swells into ear and leaves below
The May-month wild flowers and their gaudy show . . .

[. . .]

The mowing gangs bend o'er the beaded grass,
Where oft the gypsy's hungry journeying ass
Will turn its wishes from the meadow paths,
List'ning the rustle of the falling swaths.
The ploughman sweats along the fallow vales
And down the sun-cracked furrow slowly trails,
Oft seeking when athirst the brook's supply
Where, brushing eager the brink's bushes by
For coolest water, he disturbs the rest
Of ring-dove brooding o'er its idle nest.
The shepherd's leisure hours are over now;
No more he loiters 'neath the hedge-row bough
On shadow-pillowed banks and lolling stile;
The wilds must lose their summer friend awhile.
With whistle, barking dogs and chiding scold,
He drives the bleating sheep from fallow fold
To wash-pools where the willow shadows lean,
Dashing them in, their fold-stained coats to clean;
Then on the sunny sward when dry again,
He brings them homeward to the clipping pen,
Of hurdles formed, where elm or sycamore
Shut out the sun – or to some threshing-floor.
There with the scraps of songs and laugh and tale,
They lighten annual toil while merry ale
Goes round and glads some old man's heart to praise
The threadbare customs of the bygone days . . .

from Pleasures of Spring

. . . The boy near mends his pace but soodles on
Blessing the moonlight when the day is gone
And even dares to pause amid the shade
Of the old ruined castle undismayed
To mark the change – that some few weeks ago
Hid its blank walls in draperies of snow,
Marking in joy on its once naked tower
Snub elders greening and full many a flower
Of bloodwalls glowing with rich tawny streaks
Blushing in beauty from the gaping creeks,
Swathy yet lovely by each zephyr fanned
As the soft cheeks of maidens summer tanned,
Wreaths nature loves round ruin's brows to bind
From seeds took hither by the birds and wind.
He views those garlands and seems struck the while
That things so abject should be seen to smile,
Oft turning to the moon a wandering eye
That seems to journey with him through the sky,
Moves as he moves and stops as glad the while
To wait its leisure while he climbs a stile.
He walks it walks and keeps his every pace,
Runs when he runs and glories in the race.
He tries his utmost speed to leave behind
His shining friend, and thinks he beats the wind
For swiftness as he pants and hurries on,
Inly exulting that the race is won,
But spite of every vale and weary hill
He passed and climbed so swift, it followed still
And while he hums over each old tune he loves,
Do as he will it moveth as he moves
Swift as his thoughts. His speed is all in vain.
He turns to look and there it is again,
Plump opposite him, gleaming pale and wan,

As near as when his eager race began.
He thinks on the long ways he left behind
And vain wild notions fill his puzzled mind:
The gossip tales that winter did supply
Urge their faint shadows on his gazing eye,
And the pale shades that cloud the moon so wan
His artless fancies fashion to a man.
Oft has he heard, at night, when toil was done,
Rude tales of giants dwelling in the moon
And this as one of those his mind supplies
That takes his nightly journeys through the skies.
So here he stops nor urges speed again,
Deeming a race with giants doubly vain.

from Childhood

The morn when we first went to school,
Who can forget the morn? –
When the birch-whip lay upon the clock
And our hornbook it was torn.
We tore the little pictures out,
Less fond of books than play,
And only took one letter home
And that the letter 'A'.

I love in childhood's little book
To read its lessons through,
And o'er each pictured page to look
Because they read so true;
And there my heart creates anew
Love for each trifling thing
– Who can disdain the meanest weed
That shows its face in spring?

The daisy looks up in my face
As long ago it smiled;
It knows no change, but keeps its place
And takes me for a child.
The chaffinch in the hedgerow thorn
Cries 'pink pink pink' to hear
My footsteps in the early morn
As though a boy was near.

I seek no more the finch's nest,
Nor stoop for daisy flowers;
I grow a stranger to myself
In these delightful hours,
Yet when I hear the voice of spring
I can but call to mind

The pleasures which they used to bring,
The joys I used to find.

The firetail on the orchard wall
Keeps at its startled cry
Of 'tweet tut tut,' nor sees the morn
Of boyhood's mischief by;
It knows no change of changing time
By sickness never stung,
It feeds on hope's eternal prime
Around its brooded young.

Ponds where we played at 'Duck and Drake',
Where the ash with ivy grew,
Where we robbed the owl of all her eggs
And mocked her as she flew;
The broad tree in the spinney hedge
'Neath which the gypsies lay,
where we our fine oak apples got
on the twenty-ninth of May:

these all remain as then they were
and are not changed a day,
and the ivy's crown as near to green
as mine is to the grey;
it shades the pond, o'er hangs the stile;
and the oak is in the glen –
but the paths of joy are so worn out
I can't find one again . . .

Ballad – The Backward Spring

The day waxes warmer,
The winter's far gone,
Then come out my charmer
And bring summer on;
Thy beauty is gleaming
So sweet where ye be,
'Tis summer and sunshine
To be only with thee.

Tardy spring came so loathing
I thought that the spring
Had took winter's clothing,
But no such a thing;
For the snow 'neath the hedges
Hath packed up and gone
And may's little pledges
For summer comes on.

The flowers on the 'awthorn
– Oak balls on the tree
And the blackbird is building
Love's palace in glee;
Then come out my charmer
And lead summer on:
Where e'er thou art smiling
Care and winter are gone.

Even snows 'neath thy feet
I could fancy to be
A carpet of daisies
– The rime on the tree
Would bloom in thy smiling
And quickly appear

Like blossoms beguiling
The prime of the year.

The ice on the water
O I could agree
That winter had changed to
A palace for thee,
Turning pools into mirrors
And silence to glee,
Reflecting the image
Of rapture in thee.

Then come forth my charmer;
Thy presence can charm
Into summer the winter,
To sunshine the storm.
I can think how delightful
The prospect would be
In summer or winter
That blest me with thee.

But the place of thy absence
All language is lost;
I cannot imagine
What pain it would cost.
Though without thee I feel
Where a desert would be
And all in thy presence
Grows Eden with me.

The Moorhen's Nest

O poesy's power, thou overpowering sweet
That renders hearts that love thee all unmeet
For this rude world its trouble and its care,
Loading the heart with joys it cannot bear
That warms and chills and burns and bursts at last
O'er broken hopes and troubles never past,
I pay thee worship at a rustic shrine
And dream o'er joys I still imagine mine;
I pick up flowers and pebbles and by thee
As gems and jewels they appear to me;
I pick out pictures round the fields that lie
In my mind's heart like things that cannot die,
Like picking hopes and making friends with all.
Yet glass will often bear a harder fall:
As bursting bottles lose the precious wine,
Hope's casket breaks and I the gems resign;
Pain shadows on till feeling's self decays
And all such pleasures leave me is their praise.
And thus each fairy vision melts away
Like evening landscapes from the face of day,
Till hope returns with April's dewy reign,
And then I start and seek for joys again
And pick her fragments up to herd anew
Like fairy-riches pleasure loves to view,
And these associations of the past
Like summer pictures in a winter blast
Renews my heart to feelings as the rain
Falls on the earth and bids it thrive again.
Then e'en the fallow fields appear so fair,
The very weeds make sweetest gardens there
And summer there puts garments on so gay
I hate the plough that comes to disarray
Her holiday delights – and labour's toil

Seems vulgar curses on the sunny soil
And man the only object that distrains
Earth's garden into deserts for his gains.
Leave him his schemes of gain – 'tis wealth to me
Wild heaths to trace, and note their broken tree
Which lightning shivered and which nature tries
To keep alive for poesy to prize,
Upon whose mossy roots my leisure sits
To hear the birds pipe o'er their amorous fits,
Though less beloved for singing than the taste
They have to choose such homes upon the waste –
Rich architects! – and then the spots to see
How picturesque their dwellings make them be:
The wild romances of the poet's mind
No sweeter pictures for their tales can find.
And so I glad my heart and rove along,
Now finding nests, then listening to a song,
Then drinking fragrance whose perfuming cheats
Tinges life's sours and bitters into sweets,
That heart-stirred fragrance when the summer rain
Lays the road dust and sprouts the grass again,
Filling the cracks up on the beaten paths
And breathing incense from the mower's swaths,
Incense the bards and prophets of old days
Met in the wilderness to glad their praise;
And in these summer walks I seem to feel
These bible-pictures in their essence steal
Around me – and the ancientness of joy
Breathe from the woods till pleasures even cloy,
Yet holy-breathing manna seemly falls
With angel answers if a trouble calls.
And then I walk and swing my stick for joy
And catch at little pictures passing by:
A gate whose posts are two old dotterel trees,
A close with molehills sprinkled o'er its leas,
A little footbrig with its crossing rail,

A wood-gap stopped with ivy-wreathing pale,
A crooked stile each path-crossed spinney owns,
A brooklet forded by its stepping stones,
A wood-bank mined with rabbit holes – and then
An old oak leaning o'er a badger's den
Whose cave-mouth enters 'neath the twisted charms
Of its old roots and keeps it safe from harms,
Pickaxes, spades, and all its strength confounds
When hunted foxes hide from chasing hounds.
Then comes the meadows where I love to see
A flood-washed bank support an aged tree
Whose roots are bare, yet some with foothold good
Crankle and spread and strike beneath the flood,
Yet still it leans, as safer hold to win
On t'other side, and seems as tumbling in,
While every summer finds it green and gay
And winter leaves it safe as did the may.
Nor does the moorhen find its safety vain,
For on its roots their last year's homes remain,
And once again a couple from the brood
Seek their old birthplace and in safety's mood
Lodge there their flags and lay – though danger comes,
It dares and tries and cannot reach their homes –
And so they hatch their eggs and sweetly dream
On their shelfed nests that bridge the gulfy stream,
And soon the sooty brood from fear elopes
Where bulrush forests give them sweeter hopes,
Their hanging nest that aids their wishes well
Each leaves for water as it leaves the shell,
And dive and dare and every gambol try
Till they themselves to other scenes can fly.

Remembrances

Summer pleasures they are gone, like to visions every one,
And the cloudy days of autumn and of winter cometh on:
I tried to call them back, but unbidden they are gone
Far away from heart and eye and for ever far away,
Dear heart, and can it be that such raptures meet decay?
I thought them all eternal when by Langley Bush I lay;
I thought them joys eternal when I used to shout and play
On its bank at 'clink and bandy', 'chock' and 'taw' and
    ducking-stone,
Where silence sitteth now on the wild heath as her own
Like a ruin of the past all alone.

When I used to lie and sing by old Eastwell's boiling spring,
When I used to tie the willow boughs together for a 'swing'
And fish with crooked pins and thread and never catch a
    thing,
With heart just like a feather – now as heavy as a stone.
When beneath old Lea Close Oak I the bottom branches
    broke
To make our harvest cart, like so many working folk,
And then to cut a straw at the brook to have a soak,
O I never dreamed of parting or that trouble had a sting
Or that pleasures like a flock of birds would ever take to wing,
Leaving nothing but a little naked spring.

When jumping time away on old Crossberry Way
And eating 'awes like sugar-plums ere they had lost the may,
And skipping like a leveret before the peep of day
On the roly-poly up and downs of pleasant Swordy Well,
When in Round Oak's narrow lane as the south got black
    again
We sought the hollow ash that was shelter from the rain
With our pockets full of peas we had stolen from the grain,
How delicious was the dinner time on such a showery day –

O words are poor receipts for what time hath stole away,
The ancient pulpit trees and the play.

When for school o'er 'Little Field' with its brook and wooden
      brig
Where I swaggered like a man though I was not half so big,
While I held my little plough though 'twas but a willow twig,
And drove my team along made of nothing but a name –
'Gee hep' and 'hoit' and 'woi' – O I never call to mind
Those pleasant names of places but I leave a sigh behind,
While I see the little mouldywarps hang sweeing to the wind
On the only aged willow that in all the field remains,
And nature hides her face while they're sweeing in their chains
And in a silent murmuring complains.

Here was commons for their hills where they seek for freedom
      still,
Though every common's gone and though traps are set to kill
The little homeless miners – O it turns my bosom chill
When I think of old 'Sneap Green', Paddock's Nook and Hilly
      Snow
Where bramble bushes grew and the daisy gemmed in dew
And the hills of silken grass like to cushions to the view,
Where we threw the pismire crumbs when we'd nothing else
      to do –
All levelled like a desert by the never-weary plough,
All banished like the sun where that cloud is passing now,
And settled here for ever on its brow.

O I never thought that joys would run away from boys
Or that boys should change their minds and forsake such
      summer joys,
But alack I never dreamed that the world had other toys
To petrify first feelings like the fable into stone,
Till I found the pleasure past and a winter come at last –
Then the fields were sudden bare and the sky got overcast
And boyhood's pleasing haunts like a blossom in the blast

Was shrivelled to a withered weed and trampled down and
    done,
Till vanished was the morning spring and set the summer sun
And winter fought her battle-strife and won.

By Langley Bush I roam, but the bush hath left its hill;
On Cowper Green I stray, 'tis a desert strange and chill;
And spreading Lea Close Oak, ere decay had penned its will,
To the axe of the spoiler and self-interest fell a prey;
And Crossberry Way and old Round Oak's narrow lane
With its hollow trees like pulpits, I shall never see again:
Enclosure like a Bonaparte let not a thing remain,
It levelled every bush and tree and levelled every hill
And hung the moles for traitors – though the brook is
    running still,
It runs a naked stream, cold and chill.

O had I known as then joy had left the paths of men,
I had watched her night and day, be sure, and never slept
    again,
And when she turned to go, O I'd caught her mantle then
And wooed her like a lover by my lonely side to stay,
Ay, knelt and worshipped on as love in beauty's bower,
And clung upon her smiles as a bee upon a flower,
And gave her heart my poesies all cropped in a sunny hour
As keepsakes and pledges all to never fade away –
But love never heeded to treasure up the may,
So it went the common road with decay.

The Fern Owl's Nest

The weary woodman, rocking home beneath
His tightly banded faggot, wonders oft
While crossing over the furze-crowded heath
To hear the fern owl's cry that whews aloft
In circling whirls, and often by his head
Wizzes as quick as thought and ill at rest,
As through the rustling ling with heavy tread
He goes, nor heeds he tramples near its nest
That underneath the furze or squatting thorn
Lies hidden on the ground, and teazing round
That lonely spot she wakes her jarring noise
To the unheeding waste, till mottled morn
Fills the red east with daylight's coming sounds
And the heath's echoes mock the herding boys.

Swordy Well

I've loved thee, Swordy Well, and love thee still:
Long was I with thee, tenting sheep and cow
In boyhood, ramping up each steepy hill
To play at 'roly poly' down – and now
A man I trifle o'er thee, cares to kill,
Haunting thy mossy steeps to botanise
And hunt the orchis tribes where nature's skill
Doth like my thoughts run into fantasies –
Spider and bee all mimicking at will,
Displaying powers that fools the proudly wise,
Showing the wonders of great nature's plan
In trifles insignificant and small,
Puzzling the power of that great trifle man,
Who finds no reason to be proud at all.

Emmonsails Heath in Winter

I love to see the old heath's withered brake
Mingle its crimpled leaves with furze and ling
While the old heron from the lonely lake
Starts slow and flaps his melancholy wing
And oddling crow in idle motions swing
On the half-rotten ash tree's topmost twig
Beside whose trunk the gypsy makes his bed –
Up flies the bouncing woodcock from the brig
Where a black quagmire quakes beneath the tread;
The fieldfare chatters in the whistling thorn
And for the 'awe round fields and closen rove,
And coy bumbarrels twenty in a drove
Flit down the hedgerows in the frozen plain
And hang on little twigs and start again.

The Fallen Elm

Old elm that murmured in our chimney top
The sweetest anthem autumn ever made
And into mellow whispering calms would drop
When showers fell on thy many-coloured shade
And when dark tempests mimic thunder made
While darkness came as it would strangle light
With the black tempest of a winter night
That rocked thee like a cradle to thy root,
How did I love to hear the winds upbraid
Thy strength without – while all within was mute.
It seasoned comfort to our hearts' desire,
We felt thy kind protection like a friend
And edged our chairs up closer to the fire,
Enjoying comforts that was never penned.
Old favourite tree, thou'st seen times changes lower,
Though change till now did never injure thee,
For time beheld thee as her sacred dower
And nature claimed thee her domestic tree;
Storms came and shook thee many a weary hour,
Yet steadfast to thy home thy roots hath been;
Summers of thirst parched round thy homely bower
Till earth grew iron – still thy leaves was green.
The childern sought thee in thy summer shade
And made their playhouse rings of sticks and stone;
The mavis sang and felt himself alone
While in thy leaves his early nest was made
And I did feel his happiness mine own,
Nought heeding that our friendship was betrayed –
Friend not inanimate, though stocks and stones
There are and many formed of flesh and bones,
Thou owned a language by which hearts are stirred
Deeper than by a feeling clothed in words,
And speakest now what's known of every tongue,

Language of pity and the force of wrong.
What cant assumes, what hypocrites will dare,
Speaks home to truth and shows it what they are.
I see a picture which thy fate displays
And learn a lesson from thy destiny:
Self-interest saw thee stand in freedom's ways,
So thy old shadow must a tyrant be;
Thou'st heard the knave abusing those in power,
Bawl freedom loud and then oppress the free;
Thou'st sheltered hypocrites in many a shower
That when in power would never shelter thee;
Thou'st heard the knave supply his canting powers
With wrong's illusions when he wanted friends,
That bawled for shelter when he lived in showers
And when clouds vanished made thy shade amends –
With axe at root he felled thee to the ground
And barked of freedom. O I hate the sound!
Time hears its visions speak and age sublime
Had made thee a disciple unto time.
It grows the cant term of enslaving tools
To wrong another by the name of right;
It grows the licence of o'erbearing fools
To cheat plain honesty by force of might.
Thus came enclosure – ruin was its guide
But freedom's clapping hands enjoyed the sight
Though comfort's cottage soon was thrust aside
And workhouse prisons raised upon the site.
E'en nature's dwellings far away from men –
The common heath – became the spoilers' prey:
The rabbit had not where to make his den
And labour's only cow was drove away.
No matter – wrong was right and right was wrong
And freedom's bawl was sanction to the song.
– Such was thy ruin, music-making elm:
The rights of freedom was to injure thine.
As thou wert served, so would they overwhelm

In freedom's name the little that is mine.
And there are knaves that brawl for better laws
And cant of tyranny in stronger powers,
Who glut their vile unsatiated maws
And freedom's birthright from the weak devours.

The Blackcap

Under the twigs the blackcap hangs in vain
With snow-white patch streaked over either eye.
This way and that he turns, and peeps again
As wont where silk-cased insects used to lie,
But summer leaves are gone: the day is bye
For happy holidays, and now he fares
But cloudy like the weather, yet to view
He flirts a happy wing and inly wears
Content in gleaning what the orchard spares,
And like his little couzin capped in blue
Domesticates the lonely winter through
In homestead plots and gardens, where he wears
Familiar pertness – yet but seldom comes
With the tame robin to the door for crumbs.

The Landrail

How sweet and pleasant grows the way
Through summer time again,
While landrails call from day to day
Amid the grass and grain.

We hear it in the weeding time
When knee-deep waves the corn,
We hear it in the summer's prime
Through meadows, night and morn;

And now I hear it in the grass
That grows as sweet again,
And let a minute's notice pass
And now 'tis in the grain.

'Tis like a fancy everywhere,
A sort of living doubt,
We know 'tis something but it ne'er
Will blab the secret out.

If heard in close or meadow plots
It flies if we pursue,
But follows if we notice not
The close and meadow through.

Boys know the note of many a bird
In their bird-nesting rounds,
But when the landrail's noise is heard
They wonder at the sounds;

They look in every tuft of grass
That's in their rambles met,
They peep in every bush they pass
And none the wiser yet,

And still they hear the craiking sound
And still they wonder why –
It surely can't be underground
Nor is it in the sky,

And yet 'tis heard in every vale,
An undiscovered song,
And makes a pleasant wonder tale
For all the summer long.

The shepherd whistles through his hands
And starts with many a whoop
His busy dog across the lands
In hopes to fright it up.

'Tis still a minute's length or more
Till dogs are off and gone,
Then sings and louder than before
But keeps the secret on.

Yet accident will often meet
The nest within its way,
And weeders when they weed the wheat
Discover where they lay,

And mowers on the meadow lea
Chance on their noisy guest
And wonder what the bird can be
That lays without a nest.

In simple holes that birds will rake
When dusting in the ground;
They drop their eggs of curious make,
Deep-blotched and nearly round –

A mystery still to men and boys
Who knows not where they lay
And guess it but a summer noise
Among the meadow-hay.

[The Crane]

High overhead that silent throne
Of wild and cloud-betravelled sky
That makes one's loneliness more lone
Sends forth a crank and reedy cry.
I look: the crane is sailing o'er
That pathless world without a mate;
The heath looked brown and dull before
But now 'tis more than desolate.

The Wren

Why is the cuckoo's melody preferred
And nightingale's rich song so fondly praised
In poet's rhymes? Is there no other bird
Of nature's minstrelsy that oft hath raised
One's heart to ecstasy and mirth as well?
I judge not how another's taste is caught —
With mine there's other birds that bear the bell,
Whose song hath crowds of happy memories brought,
Such the wood robin singing in the dell
And little wren that many a time hath sought
Shelter from showers in huts where I did dwell
In early spring, the tenant of the plain
Tenting my sheep, and still they come to tell
The happy stories of the past again.

Wood Pictures in Spring

The rich brown-umber hue the oaks unfold
When spring's young sunshine bathes their trunks in gold,
So rich, so beautiful, so past the power
Of words to paint – my heart aches for the dower
The pencil gives to soften and infuse
This brown luxuriance of unfolding hues,
This living luscious tinting woodlands give
Into a landscape that might breathe and live,
And this old gate that claps against the tree
The entrance of spring's paradise should be –
Yet paint itself with living nature fails:
The sunshine threading through these broken rails
In mellow shades no pencil e'er conveys,
And mind alone feels fancies and portrays.

The Wryneck's Nest

That summer bird its oft-repeated note
Chirps from the dotterel ash, and in the hole
The green woodpecker made in years remote
It makes its nest – where peeping idlers strole
In anxious plundering moods – and by and by
The wryneck's curious eggs as white as snow
While squinting in the hollow tree they spy.
The sitting bird looks up with jetty eye
And waves her head in terror to and fro,
Speckled and veined in various shades of brown,
And then a hissing noise assails the clown
And quick with hasty terror in his breast
From the tree's knotty trunk he sluthers down
And thinks the strange bird guards a serpent's nest.

The Hollow Tree

How oft a summer shower hath started me
To seek for shelter in an hollow tree:
Old huge ash-dotterel wasted to a shell,
Whose vigorous head still grew and flourished well,
Where ten might sit upon the battered floor
And still look round discovering room for more,
And he who chose a hermit life to share
Might have a door and make a cabin there –
They seemed so like a house that our desires
Would call them so and make our gypsy fires
And eat field dinners of the juicy peas
Till we were wet and drabbled to the knees.
But in our old tree house, rain as it might,
Not one drop fell although it rained till night.

The Sand Martin

Thou hermit haunter of the lonely glen
And common wild and heath – the desolate face
Of rude waste landscapes far away from men
Where frequent quarries give thee dwelling place,
With strangest taste and labour undeterred
Drilling small holes along the quarry's side,
More like the haunts of vermin than a bird
And seldom by the nesting boy descried –
I've seen thee far away from all thy tribe
Flirting about the unfrequented sky
And felt a feeling that I can't describe
Of lone seclusion and a hermit joy
To see thee circle round nor go beyond
That lone heath and its melancholy pond.

The Nightingale's Nest

Up this green woodland-ride let's softly rove
And list the nightingale – she dwells just here.
Hush! let the wood-gate softly clap for fear
The noise might drive her from her home of love,
For here I've heard her many a merry year –
At morn, at eve, nay, all the livelong day,
As though she lived on song. This very spot,
Just where that old-man's-beard all wildly trails
Rude arbours o'er the road and stops the way –
And where that child its bluebell flowers hath got,
Laughing and creeping through the mossy rails –
There have I hunted like a very boy,
Creeping on hands and knees through matted thorn
To find her nest and see her feed her young.
And vainly did I many hours employ:
All seemed as hidden as a thought unborn.
And where those crimping fern-leaves ramp among
The hazel's under-boughs, I've nestled down
And watched her while she sung, and her renown
Hath made me marvel that so famed a bird
Should have no better dress than russet brown.
Her wings would tremble in her ecstasy
And feathers stand on end as 'twere with joy
And mouth wide open to release her heart
Of its out-sobbing songs. The happiest part
Of summer's fame she shared, for so to me
Did happy fancies shapen her employ,
But if I touched a bush or scarcely stirred,
All in a moment stopped. I watched in vain:
The timid bird had left the hazel bush
And at a distance hid to sing again.
Lost in a wilderness of listening leaves,
Rich ecstasy would pour its luscious strain

Till envy spurred the emulating thrush
To start less wild and scarce inferior songs,
For while of half the year care him bereaves
To damp the ardour of his speckled breast,
The nightingale to summer's life belongs
And naked trees and winter's nipping wrongs
Are strangers to her music and her rest.
Her joys are evergreen, her world is wide –
Hark! there she is as usual – let's be hush –
For in this blackthorn-clump, if rightly guessed,
Her curious house is hidden. Part aside
These hazel branches in a gentle way
And stoop right cautious 'neath the rustling boughs,
For we will have another search today
And hunt this fern-strewn thorn clump round and round,
And where this seeded wood-grass idly bows
We'll wade right through, it is a likely nook:
In such like spots and often on the ground,
They'll build, where rude boys never think to look.
Ay, as I live – her secret nest is here,
Upon this whitethorn stulp. I've searched about
For hours in vain – there, put that bramble by –
Nay, trample on its branches and get near.
How subtle is the bird! she started out
And raised a plaintive note of danger nigh
Ere we were past the brambles, and now, near
Her nest, she sudden stops – as choking fear
That might betray her home. So even now
We'll leave it as we found it: safety's guard
Of pathless solitudes shall keep it still.
See there – she's sitting on the old oak bough,
Mute in her fears; our presence doth retard
Her joys, and doubt turns every rapture chill.
Sing on, sweet bird, may no worse hap befall
Thy visions than the fear that now deceives.
We will not plunder music of its dower

Nor turn this spot of happiness to thrall,
For melody seems hid in every flower
That blossoms near thy home – these harebells all
Seem bowing with the beautiful in song
And gaping cuckoo-flower with spotted leaves
Seems blushing with the singing it has heard.
How curious is the nest: no other bird
Uses such loose materials or weaves
Its dwelling in such spots – dead oaken leaves
Are placed without and velvet moss within
And little scraps of grass and, scant and spare,
What scarcely seem materials, down and hair.
For from man's haunts she nothing seems to win,
Yet nature is the builder and contrives
Homes for her children's comfort even here
Where solitude's disciples spend their lives
Unseen, save when a wanderer passes near
That loves such pleasant places. Deep adown
The nest is made, a hermit's mossy cell.
Snug lie her curious eggs in number five
Of deadened green or rather olive-brown,
And the old prickly thorn-bush guards them well.
So here we'll leave them, still unknown to wrong,
As the old woodland's legacy of song.

Insects

Thou tiney loiterer on the barley's beard
And happy unit of a numerous herd
Of playfellows the laughing summer brings
Mocking the sunshine in their glittering wings.
How merrily they creep and run and fly;
No kin they bear to labour's drudgery,
Smoothing the velvet of the pale hedge rose,
And where they fly for dinner no one knows;
The dewdrops feed them not – they love the shine
Of noon, whose sun may bring them golden wine.
All day they're playing in their Sunday dress
Till night goes sleep and they can do no less,
Then in the heath bell's silken hood they fly
And like to princes in their slumber lie
From coming night and dropping dews and all,
In silken beds and roomy painted hall.
So happily they spend their summer day,
Now in the corn fields, now the new mown hay.
One almost fancies that such happy things
In coloured hoods and richly burnished wings
Are fairy folk in splendid masquerade
Disguised through fear, of mortal folk afraid,
Keeping their merry pranks a mystery still
Lest glaring day should do their secrets ill.

The Eternity of Nature

Leaves from eternity are simple things
To the world's gaze – whereto a spirit clings
Sublime and lasting. Trampled underfoot,
The daisy lives and strikes its little root
Into the lap of time: centuries may come
And pass away into the silent tomb
And still the child hid in the womb of time
Shall smile and pluck them when this simple rhyme
Shall be forgotten like a churchyard stone
Or lingering lie unnoticed and alone.
When eighteen hundred years, our common date,
Grow many thousands in their marching state,
Ay, still the child with pleasure in his eye
Shall cry – the daisy! a familiar cry –
And run to pluck it, in the self-same state
As when time found it in his infant date
And like a child himself when all was new
Might smile with wonder and take notice too.
Its little golden bosom frilled with snow
Might win e'en Eve to stoop adown and show
Her partner Adam in the silky grass
This little gem that smiled where pleasure was
And, loving Eve, from Eden followed ill
And bloomed with sorrow and lives smiling still.

As once in Eden under heaven's breath,
So now on earth and on the lap of death
It smiles for ever. Cowslips' golden blooms
That in the closen and the meadow comes
Shall come when kings and empires fade and die,
And in the meadows as time's partners lie
As fresh two thousand years to come as now,
With those five crimson spots upon its brow.

And little brooks that hum a simple lay
In green unnoticed spots, from praise away,
Shall sing when poets in time's darkness hid
Shall lie like memory in a pyramid,
Forgetting yet not all forgot, though lost
Like a thread's end in ravelled windings crossed.
And the small bumble-bee shall hum as long
As nightingales, for time protects the song;
And nature is their soul, to whom all clings
Of fair or beautiful in lasting things.
The little robin in the quiet glen,
Hidden from fame and all the strife of men,
Sings unto time a pastoral and gives
A music that lives on and ever lives.
Both spring and autumn years rich bloom and fade,
Longer than songs that poets ever made.
And think ye these time's playthings? Pass, proud skill,
Time loves them like a child and ever will,
And so I worship them in bushy spots
And sing with them when all else notice not,
And feel the music of their mirth agree
With that sooth quiet that bestirs in me.
And if I touch aright that quiet tone,
That soothing truth that shadows forth their own,
Then many a year shall grow in after-days
And still find hearts to love my quiet lays.
Yet cheering mirth with thoughts sung not for fame
But for the joy that with their utterance came,
That inward breath of rapture urged not loud –
Birds, singing lone, fly silent past a crowd –
So in these pastoral spots which childish time
Makes dear to me, I wander out and rhyme.
What time the dewy morning's infancy
Hangs on each blade of grass and every tree,
And sprents the red thighs of the bumble-bee
Who 'gins betimes unwearied minstrelsy,

Who breakfasts, dines and most divinely sups
With every flower save golden buttercups –
On their proud bosoms he will never go
And passes by with scarcely 'How do ye do?'
So in their showy shining gaudy cells
Maybe the summer's honey never dwells.
Her ways are mysteries: all yet endless youth
Lives in them all, unchangeable as truth.
With the odd number five, strange nature's laws
Plays many freaks nor once mistakes the cause;
And in the cowslip-peeps this very day
Five spots appear, which time ne'er wears away
Nor once mistakes the counting – look within
Each peep, and five, nor more nor less, is seen.
And trailing bindweed with its pinky cup
Five leaves of paler hue goes streaking up;
And birds a many keep the rule alive
And lay five eggs, nor more nor less than five.
And flowers, how many own that mystic power
With five leaves ever making up the flower!
The five-leaved grass, trailing its golden cup
Of flowers – five leaves make all for which I stoop.
And bryony in the hedge that now adorns
The tree to which it clings, and now the thorns,
Owns five-starred pointed leaves of dingy white;
Count which I will, all make the number right.
And spreading goose-grass, trailing all abroad
In leaves of silver green about the road –
Five leaves make every blossom all along.
I stoop for many, none are counted wrong.
'Tis nature's wonder and her maker's will,
Who bade earth be and order owns him still,
As that superior power who keeps the key
Of wisdom, power and might through all eternity.

Emmonsales Heath

In thy wild garb of other times
I find thee lingering still;
Furze o'er each lazy summit climbs
At nature's easy will.

Grasses that never knew a scythe
Wave all the summer long;
And wild weed blossoms waken blithe,
That ploughmen never wrong.

Stern industry with stubborn toil
And wants unsatisfied
Still leaves untouched thy maiden soil
In its unsullied pride.

The birds still find their summer shades
To build their nests again,
And the poor hare its rushy glade
To hide from savage men.

Nature its family protects
In thy security,
And blooms that love what man neglects
Find peaceful homes in thee.

The wild rose scents the summer air
And woodbines weave in bowers
To glad the swain sojourning there
And maidens gathering flowers.

Creation's steps one's wandering meets
Untouched by those of man:
Things seem the same in such retreats
As when the world began.

Furze, ling and brake all mingling free
And grass for ever green –
All seem the same old things to be
As they have ever been.

The dyke o'er such neglected ground,
One's weariness to soothe,
Still wildly winds its lawless bound
And chafes the pebble smooth,

Crooked and rude as when at first
Its waters learned to stray
And from their mossy fountain burst,
It washed itself a way.

O who can pass such lovely spots
Without a wish to stray
And leave life's cares awhile forgot
To muse an hour away?

I've often met with places rude,
Nor failed their sweets to share,
But passed an hour with solitude
And left my blessing there.

He that can meet the morning wind
And o'er such places roam,
Nor leave a lingering wish behind
To make their peace his home –

His heart is dead to quiet hours
Nor love his mind employs,
Poesy with him ne'er shares its flowers
Nor solitude its joys.

O there are spots amid thy bowers
Which nature loves to find,
Where spring drops round her earliest flowers
Unchecked by winter's wind,

Where cowslips wake the child's surprise,
Sweet peeping ere their time,
Ere April spreads her dappled skies
'Mid morning's powdered rime.

I've stretched my boyish walks to thee
When May-day's paths were dry,
When leaves had nearly hid each tree
And grass greened ankle-high,

And mused the sunny hours away
And thought of little things
That children mutter o'er their play
When fancy tries its wings.

Joy nursed me in her happy moods
And all life's little crowd
That haunt the waters, fields and woods
Would sing their joys aloud.

I thought how kind that mighty power
Must in his splendour be,
Who spread around my boyish hour
Such gleams of harmony,

Who did with joyous rapture fill
The low as well as high
And made the pismires round the hill
Seem full as blest as I.

Hope's sun is seen of every eye;
The halo that it gives
In nature's wide and common sky
Cheers everything that lives.

The Pettichap's Nest

Well, in my many walks I rarely found
A place less likely for a bird to form
Its nest – close by the rut-gulled wagon road
And on the almost bare foot-trodden ground
With scarce a clump of grass to keep it warm,
And not a thistle spreads its spears abroad
Or prickly bush to shield it from harm's way,
And yet so snugly made that none may spy
It out save accident – and you and I
Had surely passed it in our walk to day
Had chance not led us by it – nay e'en now,
Had not the old bird heard us trampling by
And fluttered out, we had not seen it lie
Brown as the roadway side – small bits of hay
Plucked from the old propped-haystack's pleachy brow
And withered leaves make up its outward walls
That from the snub-oak dotterel yearly falls
And in the old hedge-bottom rot away.
Built like a oven with a little hole
Hard to discover that snug entrance wins,
Scarcely admitting e'en two fingers in,
And lined with feathers warm as silken stole
And soft as seats of down for painless ease
And full of eggs scarce bigger e'en than peas.

Here's one most delicate with spots as small
As dust – and of a faint and pinky red.
– Well, let them be and safety guard them well
For fear's rude paths around are thickly spread
And they are left to many dangers' ways
When green grasshoppers' jumps might break the shells,
While lowing oxen pass them morn and night
And restless sheep around them hourly stray

And no grass springs but hungry horses bite,
That trample past them twenty times a day.
Yet, like a miracle, in safety's lap
They still abide unhurt and out of sight.
– Stop, here's the bird – that woodman at the gap
Hath frit it from the hedge – 'tis olive green –
Well, I declare, it is the pettichap!
Not bigger than the wren and seldom seen:
I've often found their nests in chance's way
When I in pathless woods did idly roam,
But never did I dream until today
A spot like this would be her chosen home.

The Yellowhammer's Nest

Just by the wooden brig a bird flew up,
Frit by the cowboy as he scrambled down
To reach the misty dewberry – let us stoop
And seek its nest – the brook we need not dread,
'Tis scarcely deep enough a bee to drown,
So it sings harmless o'er its pebbly bed
– Ay here it is, stuck close beside the bank
Beneath the bunch of grass that spindles rank
Its husk seeds tall and high – 'tis rudely planned
Of bleachèd stubbles and the withered fare
That last year's harvest left upon the land,
Lined thinly with the horse's sable hair.
Five eggs, pen-scribbled o'er with ink their shells
Resembling writing scrawls which fancy reads
As nature's poesy and pastoral spells –
They are the yellowhammer's and she dwells
Most poet-like where brooks and flowery weeds
As sweet as Castaly to fancy seems
And that old molehill like as Parnass' hill
On which her partner haply sits and dreams
O'er all her joys of song – so leave it still
A happy home of sunshine, flowers and streams.
Yet in the sweetest places cometh ill,
A noisome weed that burthens every soil;
For snakes are known with chill and deadly coil
To watch such nests and seize the helpless young,
And like as though the plague became a guest,
Leaving a houseless home, a ruined nest –
And mournful hath the little warblers sung
When such like woes hath rent its little breast.

The Skylark

The rolls and harrows lie at rest beside
The battered road, and spreading far and wide
Above the russet clods the corn is seen
Sprouting its spiry points of tender green
Where squats the hare, to terrors wide awake,
Like some brown clod the harrows failed to break,
While 'neath the warm hedge boys stray far from home
To crop the early blossoms as they come
Where buttercups will make them eager run,
Opening their golden caskets to the sun
To see who shall be first to pluck the prize;
And from their hurry up the skylark flies
And o'er her half-formed nest with happy wings
Winnows the air – till in the cloud she sings,
Then hangs, a dust spot in the sunny skies,
And drops and drops till in her nest she lies,
Where boys unheeding past – ne'er dreaming then
That birds which flew so high would drop again
To nests upon the ground where anything
May come at to destroy. Had they the wing
Like such a bird, themselves would be too proud
And build on nothing but a passing cloud,
As free from danger as the heavens are free
From pain and toil – there would they build and be
And sail about the world to scenes unheard
Of and unseen – O were they but a bird,
So think they while they listen to its song,
And smile and fancy and so pass along
While its low nest moist with the dews of morn
Lies safely with the leveret in the corn.

Summer Moods

I love at eventide to walk alone
Down narrow lanes o'erhung with dewy thorn
Where, from the long grass underneath, the snail
Jet black creeps out and sprouts his timid horn.
I love to muse o'er meadows newly mown
Where withering grass perfumes the sultry air,
Where bees search round with sad and weary drone
In vain for flowers that bloomed but newly there,
While in the juicy corn the hidden quail
Cries 'wet my foot' and hid as thoughts unborn
The fairylike and seldom-seen landrail
Utters 'craik craik' like voices underground,
Right glad to meet the evening's dewy veil
And see the light fade into glooms around.

Evening Schoolboys

Harken that happy shout – the schoolhouse door
Is open thrown and out the younkers teem.
Some run to leapfrog on the rushy moor
And others dabble in the shallow stream,
Catching young fish and turning pebbles o'er
For muscle clams – Look in that sunny gleam
Where the retiring sun that rests the while
Streams through the broken hedge – How happy seem
Those schoolboy friendships leaning o'er the stile,
Both reading in one book – anon a dream
Rich with new joys doth their young hearts beguile
And the books pocketed right hastily.
Ah happy boys, well may ye turn and smile
When joys are yours that never cost a sigh.

Lord Byron

A splendid sun hath set – when shall our eyes
Behold a morn so beautiful arise
As that which gave his mighty genius birth
And all eclipsed the lesser lights on earth?
His first young burst of twilight did declare
Beyond that haze a sun was rising there,
As when the morn to usher in the day
Speeds from the east in sober garb of grey
At first, till warming into wild delight
She casts her mantle off and shines in light.
The labours of small minds an age may dream
And be but shadows on time's running stream,
While genius in an hour makes what shall be
The next a portion of eternity.

To the Memory of Bloomfield

Sweet unassuming minstrel, not to thee
The dazzling fashions of the day belong:
Nature's wild pictures, field and cloud and tree
And quiet brooks far distant from the throng
In murmurs tender as the toiling bee
Make the sweet music of thy gentle song.
Well, nature owns thee: let the crowd pass by,
The tide of fashion is a stream too strong
For pastoral brooks that gently flow and sing,
But nature is their source, and earth and sky
Their annual offering to her current bring.
Thy gentle muse and memory need no sigh,
For thine shall murmur on to many a spring
When their proud streams are summer-burnt and dry.

Beans in Blossom

The south-west wind, how pleasant in the face
It breathes, while sauntering in a musing pace
I roam these new-ploughed fields, and by the side
Of this old wood where happy birds abide
And the rich blackbird through his golden bill
Utters wild music when the rest are still:
Now luscious comes the scent of blossomed beans
That o'er the path in rich disorder leans,
Mid which the bees in busy songs and toils
Load home luxuriantly their yellow spoils;
The herd cows toss the molehills in their play;
And often stand the stranger's steps at bay
Mid clover blossoms red and tawny-white,
Strong-scented with the summer's warm delight.

Sudden Shower

Black grows the southern sky betokening rain
And humming hive-bees homeward hurry by;
They feel the change – so let us shun the grain
And take the broad road while our feet are dry.
Ay, there some dropples moistened in my face
And pattered on my hat – 'tis coming nigh –
Let's look about and find a sheltering place.
The little things around, like you and I,
Are hurrying through the grass to shun the shower.
Here stoops an ash tree – hark, the wind gets high,
But never mind, this ivy for an hour,
Rain as it may, will keep us dryly here.
That little wren knows well his sheltering bower
Nor leaves his dry house though we come so near.

Pleasant Places

Old stone pits with veined ivy overhung,
Wild crooked brooks o'er which is rudely flung
A rail and plank that bends beneath the tread,
Old narrow lanes where trees meet overhead,
Path-stiles on which a steeple we espy
Peeping and stretching in the distant sky,
And heaths o'erspread with furze-bloom's sunny shine
Where wonder pauses to exclaim 'divine!'
Old ponds dim-shadowed with a broken tree –
These are the picturesque of taste to me,
While painting winds, to make complete the scene
In rich confusion mingles every green,
Waving the sketchy pencil in their hands,
Shading the living scenes to fairy lands.

The Hail Storm in June 1831

Darkness came o'er like chaos – and the sun,
As startled with the terror, seemed to run
With quickened dread behind the beetling cloud;
The old wood sung like nature in her shroud
And each old rifted oak tree's mossy arm
Seemed shrinking from the presence of the storm
And as it nearer came they shook beyond
Their former fears – as if to burst the bond
Of earth that bound them to that ancient place,
Where danger seemed to threaten all their race
Who had withstood all tempests since their birth
Yet now seemed bowing to the very earth:
Like reeds they bent, like drunken men they reeled,
Till man from shelter ran and sought the open field.

Hares at Play

The birds are gone to bed; the cows are still,
And sheep lie panting on each old mole hill,
And underneath the willow's grey-green bough –
Like toil a resting – lies the fallow plough.
The timid hares throw daylight's fears away
On the lane's road, to dust and dance and play
Then dabble in the grain, by nought deterred,
To lick the dewfall from the barley's beard,
Then out they sturt again and round the hill
Like happy thoughts – dance – squat – and loiter still
Till milking maidens in the early morn
Gingle their yokes and sturt them in the corn;
Through well known beaten paths each nimbling hare
Sturts quick as fear – and seeks its hidden lair.

The Flood

On Lolham Brigs in wild and lonely mood
I've seen the winter floods their gambols play
Through each old arch that trembled while I stood
Bent o'er its wall to watch the dashing spray;
As their old stations would be washed away
Crash came the ice against the jambs and then
A shudder jarred the arches – yet once more
It breasted raving waves and stood again
To wait the shock as stubborn as before
– While foam, brown crested with the russet soil
As washed from new ploughed lands, would dart beneath
Then round and round a thousand eddies boil
On tother side – then pause as if for breath
One minute – and ingulphed – like life in death
Whose wrecky stains dart on the floods away
More swift then shadows in a stormy day;
Things trail and turn and steady – all in vain
The engulphing arches shoot them quickly through
The feather dances, flutters, and again
Darts through the deepest dangers still afloat,
Seeming as fairies whisked it from the view
And danced it o'er the waves as pleasure's boat
Light hearted as a merry thought in May –
Trays – uptorn bushes – fence demolished rails,
Loaded with weeds in sluggish motions, stray
Like water monsters lost: each winds and trails
Till near the arches – then as in afright
It plunges – reels – and shudders out of sight.

Waves trough – rebound – and fury boil again
Like plunging monsters rising underneath
Who at the top curl up a shaggy main,
A moment catching at a surer breath,

Then plunging headlong down and down – and on
Each following boil the shadow of the last,
And other monsters rise when those are gone,
Crest their fringed waves – plunge onward and are past
– The chill air comes around me ocean blea.
From bank to bank the waterstrife is spread.
Strange birds like snow spots o'er the huzzing sea
Hang where the wild duck hurried past and fled.
On roars the flood – all restless to be free
Like trouble wandering to eternity.

Mist in the Meadows

The evening o'er the meadow seems to stoop;
More distant lessens the diminished spire.
Mist in the hollows reeks and curdles up
Like fallen clouds that spread – and things retire
Less seen and less – the shepherd passes near
And little distant most grotesquely shades
As walking without legs – lost to his knees
As through the rawky creeping smoke he wades.
Now half way up the arches dissappear
And small the bits of sky that glimmer through
Then trees loose all but tops – I meet the fields
And now the indistinctness passes by:
The shepherd all his length is seen again
And further on the village meets the eye.

from Flittings: On Leaving the Cottage of my Birth

I've left mine own old home of homes,
Green fields and every pleasant place;
The summer like a stranger comes,
I pause and hardly know her face;
I miss the hazel's happy green,
The bluebell's quiet-hanging blooms,
Where envy's sneer was never seen,
Where staring malice never comes.

I miss the heath, its yellow furze,
Molehills and rabbit tracks that lead
Through besom-ling and teasel burrs
That spread a wilderness indeed,
The woodland oaks and all below
That their white-powdered branches shield,
The mossy paths – the very crow
Croaked music in my native field.

I sit me in my corner chair
That seems to feel itself from home,
And hear bird-music here and there
From 'awthorn hedge and orchard come,
I hear but all is strange and new
– I sat on my old bench last June,
The sailing puddock's shrill 'peelew'
O'er Royce Wood seemed a sweeter tune.

I walk adown the narrow lane,
The nightingale is singing now,
But like to me she seems at loss
For Royce Wood and its shielding bough.
I lean upon the window sill,
The trees and summer happy seem,

Green, sunny green they shine – but still
My heart goes far away to dream

Of happiness, and thoughts arise
With home-bred pictures many a one:
Green lanes that shut out burning skies
And old crook'd stiles to rest upon;
Above them hangs the maple tree,
Below grass swells a velvet hill
And little footpaths sweet to see
Goes seeking sweeter places still,

With by and by a brook to cross,
O'er which a little arch is thrown.
No brook is here: I feel the loss
From home and friends and all alone.
The stone pit with its shelving sides
Seemed hanging rocks in my esteem,
I miss the prospect far and wide
From Langley Bush, and so I seem

Alone and in a stranger scene
Far far from spots my heart esteems:
The closen with their ancient green,
Heaths, woods and pastures, sunny streams.
The hawthorns here are hung with may
But still they seem in deader green;
The sun e'en seems to lose its way
Nor knows the quarter it is in.

I dwell on trifles like a child,
I feel as ill becomes a man,
And still my thoughts like weedlings wild
Grow up to blossom where they can:
They turn to places known so long
And feel that joy was dwelling there,
So homebred pleasure fills the song
That has no presentjoys to heir.

To the Snipe

Lover of swamps,
The quagmire overgrown
With hassock-tufts of sedge – where fear encamps
Around thy home alone

The trembling grass
Quakes from the human foot
Nor bears the weight of man to let him pass
Where thou alone and mute

Sittest at rest
In safety 'neath the clump
Of huge flag-forest that thy haunts invest
Or some old sallow stump

Thriving on seams
That tiny islands swell,
Just hilling from the mud and rancid streams,
Suiting thy nature well –

For here thy bill,
Suited by wisdom good
Of rude unseemly length, doth delve and drill
The gelid mass for food,

And here, mayhap,
When summer suns hath dressed
The moor's rude, desolate and spongy lap,
May hide thy mystic nest –

Mystic indeed,
For isles that ocean make
Are scarcely more secure for birds to build
Than this flag-hidden lake.

Boys thread the woods
To their remotest shades,
But in these marshy flats, these stagnant floods,
Security pervades

From year to year,
Places untrodden lie
Where man nor boy nor stock hath ventured near
– Nought gazed on but the sky

And fowl that dread
The very breath of man,
Hiding in spots that never knew his tread –
A wild and timid clan,

Widgeon and teal
And wild duck, restless lot
That from man's dreaded sight will ever steal
To the most dreary spot.

Here tempests howl
Around each flaggy plot
Where they who dread man's sight, the waterfowl,
Hide and are frighted not.

'Tis power divine
That heartens them to brave
The roughest tempest and at ease recline
On marshes or the wave;

Yet instinct knows
Not safety's bounds – to shun
The firmer ground where stalking fowler goes
With searching dogs and gun

By tepid springs
Scarcely one stride across:
Though brambles from its edge a shelter flings,
Thy safety is at loss.

And never choose
The little sinky foss
Streaking the moors whence spa-red water spews
From puddles fringed with moss:

Freebooters there,
Intent to kill or slay,
Startle with cracking guns the trepid air
And dogs thy haunts betray.

From danger's reach
Here thou art safe to roam
Far as these washy flag-sown marshes stretch,
A still and quiet home.

In these thy haunts
I've gleaned habitual love;
From the vague world where pride and folly taunts
I muse and look above.

Thy solitudes
The unbounded heaven esteems
And here my heart warms into higher moods
And dignifying dreams.

I see the sky
Smile on the meanest spot,
Giving to all that creep or walk or fly
A calm and cordial lot.

Thine teaches me
Right feelings to employ:
That in the dreariest places peace will be
A dweller and a joy.

[The Lament of Swordy Well]

Petitioners are full of prayers
To fall in pity's way,
But if her hand the gift forbears
They'll sooner swear than pray.
They're not the worst to want, who lurch
On plenty with complaints,
No more than those who go to church
Are e'er the better saints.

I hold no hat to beg a mite
Nor pick it up when thrown,
No limping leg I hold in sight
But pray to keep my own.
Where profit gets his clutches in,
There's little he will leave;
Gain stooping for a single pin
Will stick it on his sleeve.

For passers-by I never pin
No troubles to my breast,
Nor carry round some names to win
More money from the rest.
I'm Swordy Well, a piece of land
That's fell upon the town,
Who worked me till I couldn't stand
And crush me now I'm down.

In parish bonds I well may wail,
Reduced to every shift;
Pity may grieve at trouble's tale
But cunning shares the gift.
Harvests with plenty on his brow
Leaves losses'taunts with me,
Yet gain comes yearly with the plough
And will not let me be.

Alas dependence, thou'rt a brute
Want only understands;
His feelings wither branch and root
That falls in parish hands.
The muck that clouts the ploughman's shoe,
The moss that hides the stone,
Now I'm become the parish due
Is more than I can own.

Though I'm no man, yet any wrong
Some sort of right may seek,
And I am glad if e'en a song
Gives me the room to speak.
I've got among such grubbling gear
And such a hungry pack,
If I brought harvests twice a year
They'd bring me nothing back.

When war their tyrant prices got,
I trembled with alarms;
They fell and saved my little spot,
Or towns had turned to farms.
Let profit keep an humble place
That gentry may be known;
Let pedigrees their honours trace
And toil enjoy its own.

The silver springs grown naked dykes
Scarce own a bunch of rushes;
When grain got high the tasteless tykes
Grubbed up trees, banks and bushes,
And me, they turned me inside out
For sand and grit and stones
And turned my old green hills about
And picked my very bones.

These things that claim my own as theirs
Were born but yesterday,

But ere I fell to town affairs
I were as proud as they:
I kept my horses, cows and sheep
And built the town below
Ere they had cat or dog to keep –
And then to use me so.

Parish allowance, gaunt and dread,
Had it the earth to keep,
Would even pine the bees to dead
To save an extra keep.
Pride's workhouse is a place that yields
From poverty its gains,
And mine's a workhouse for the fields,
A-starving the remains.

The bees fly round in feeble rings
And find no blossom by,
Then thrum their almost-weary wings
Upon the moss and die.
Rabbits that find my hills turned o'er
Forsake my poor abode –
They dread a workhouse like the poor
And nibble on the road.

If with a clover bottle now
Spring dares to lift her head,
The next day brings the hasty plough
And makes me misery's bed.
The butterflies may whirr and come,
I cannot keep 'em now,
Nor can they bear my parish home
That withers on my brow.

No, now not e'en a stone can lie,
I'm just whate'er they like;
My hedges like the winter fly
And leave me but the dyke;

My gates are thrown from off the hooks,
The parish thoroughfare:
Lord, he that's in the parish books
Has little wealth to spare.

I couldn't keep a dust of grit
Nor scarce a grain of sand,
But bags and carts claimed every bit
And now they've got the land.
I used to bring the summer's life
To many a butterfly,
But in oppression's iron strife
Dead tussocks bow and sigh.

I've scarce a nook to call my own
For things that creep or fly –
The beetle hiding 'neath a stone
Does well to hurry by.
Stock eats my struggles every day
As bare as any road;
He's sure to be in something's way
If e'er he stirs abroad.

I am no man to whine and beg,
But fond of freedom still
I hang no lies on pity's peg
To bring a grist to mill;
On pity's back I needn't jump,
My looks speak loud alone –
My only tree they've left a stump
And nought remains my own.

My mossy hills gain's greedy hand
And more than greedy mind
Levels into a russet land,
Nor leaves a bent behind.
In summers gone I bloomed in pride,
Folks came for miles to prize

My flowers that bloomed nowhere beside
And scarce believed their eyes.

Yet worried with a greedy pack
They rend and delve and tear
The very grass from off my back –
I've scarce a rag to wear,
Gain takes my freedom all away
Since its dull suit I wore
And yet scorn vows I never pay
And hurts me more and more.

Whoever pays me rent or takes it,
I've neither words or dates;
One makes the law and others break it
And stop my mouth with rates.

And should the price of grain get high –
Lord help and keep it low –
I shan't possess a single fly
Or get a weed to grow;
I shan't possess a yard of ground
To bid a mouse to thrive,
For gain has put me in a pound,
I scarce can keep alive.

I'm not a man, as some may think,
Petitioning for loss
Of cow that died of age's drink
And spavin-foundered horse
For which some beg a list of pelf
And seem on loss to thrive,
But I petition for myself
And beg to keep alive.

There's folks that make a mort of bother
And o'er lost gainings whine,
But, lord, of me I'm this and t'other,

There's no one cares for mine.
They strip the grass from off my back
And take my things away:
I'm robbed by every outlaw pack
[   ]

I own I'm poor like many more
But then the poor mun live,
And many came for miles before
For what I had to give;
But since I fell upon the town
They pass me with a sigh,
I've scarce the room to say 'Sit down'
And so they wander by.

The town that brought me in disgrace
Have got their tales to say;
I ha'n't a friend in all the place
Save one and he's away.
A grubbling man with much to keep
And nought to keep 'em on
Found me a bargain offered cheap
And so my peace was gone.

But when a poor man is allowed
So to enslave another,
Well may the world's tongue prate aloud
How brother uses brother.
I could not keep a bush to stand
For years but what was gone,
And now I ha'n't a foot of land
To keep a rabbit on.

They used to come and feed at night
When danger's day was gone,
And in the morning out of sight
Hide underneath a stone.

I'm fain to shun the greedy pack
That now so tear and brag;
They strip the coat from off my back
And scarcely leave a rag,
That like the parish hurt and hurt
While gain's new suit I wear,
Then swear I never pay 'em for't
And add to my despair.

Though now I seem so full of clack,
Yet when you're riding by
The very birds upon my back
Are not more fain to fly.
I feel so lorn in this disgrace,
God send the grain to fall;
I am the oldest in the place
And the worst-served of all.

Lord bless ye, I was kind to all
And poverty in me
Could always find a humble stall,
A rest and lodging free;
Poor bodies with an hungry ass
I welcomed many a day,
And gave him tether-room and grass
And never said him nay.

There was a time my bit of ground
Made freemen of the slave;
The ass no pindar'd dare to pound
When I his supper gave;
The gypsies' camp was not afraid,
I made his dwelling free,
Till vile enclosure came and made
A parish slave of me.

The gypsies further on sojourn,
No parish bonds they like;
No sticks I own, and would earth burn
I shouldn't own a dyke.
I am no friend to lawless work,
Nor would a rebel be,
And why I call a Christian Turk
Is they are Turks to me.

I am the last
Of all the field that fell;
My name is nearly all that's left
Of what was Swordy Well.

And if I could but find a friend
With no deceit to sham,
Who'd send me some few sheep to tend
And leave me as I am,
To keep my hills from cart and plough
And strife of mongrel men
And as spring found me find me now,
I should look up again.

And save his Lordship's woods that past
The day of danger dwell,
Of all the fields I am the last
That my own face can tell.
Yet, what with stone pits' delving holes
And strife to buy and sell,
My name will quickly be the whole
That's left of Swordy Well.

Snowstorm

What a night: the wind howls, hisses and but stops
To howl more loud while the snow volley keeps
Incessant batter at the window pane,
Making our comfort feel as sweet again;
And in the morning, when the tempest drops,
At every cottage door mountainous heaps
Of snow lies drifted, that all entrance stops
Until the besom and the shovel gains
The path – and leaves a wall on either side.
The shepherd, rambling valleys white and wide,
With new sensations his old memories fills
When hedges left at night no more descried
Are turned to one white sweep of curving hills
And trees turned bushes half their bodies hide.

Bumbarrel's Nest

The oddling bush, close sheltered hedge new-plashed,
Of which spring's early liking makes a guest
First with a shade of green though winter-dashed –
There, full as soon, bumbarrels make a nest
Of mosses grey with cobwebs closely tied
And warm and rich as feather-bed within,
With little hole on its contrary side
That pathway peepers may no knowledge win
Of what her little oval nest contains –
Ten eggs and often twelve, with dusts of red
Soft frittered – and full soon the little lanes
Screen the young crowd and hear the twitt'ring song
Of the old birds who call them to be fed
While down the hedge they hang and hide along.

[November]

The shepherds almost wonder where they dwell
And the old dog for his night journey stares:
The path leads somewhere but they cannot tell
And neighbour meets with neighbour unawares.
The maiden passes close beside her cow
And wonders on and thinks her far away.
The ploughman goes unseen behind his plough
And seems to loose his horses half the day.
The lazy mist creeps on in journey slow;
The maidens shout and wonder where they go.
So dull and dark are the November days,
The lazy mist high up the evening curled,
And now the morn quite hides in smokey haze:
The place we occupy seems all the world.

Open Winter

Where slanting banks are always with the sun
The daisy is in blossom even now
And where warm patches by the hedges run
The cottager when coming home from plough
Brings home a cowslip root in flower to set;
Thus ere the Christmas goes the spring is met
Setting up little tents about the fields
In sheltered spots – primroses when they get
Behind the wood's old roots where ivy shields
Their crimpled curdled leaves will shine and hide
– Cart ruts and horse footings scarcely yield
A slur for boys just crizzled and that's all.
Frost shoots his needles by the small dyke side
And snow in scarce a feather's seen to fall.

[sonnet sequence on Fox and Badger]

The shepherd on his journey heard when nigh
His dog among the bushes barking high;
The ploughman ran and gave a hearty shout,
He found a weary fox and beat him out.
The ploughman laughed and would have ploughed him in,
But the old shepherd took him for the skin.
He lay upon the furrow stretched and dead,
The old dog lay and licked the wounds that bled,
The ploughman beat him till his ribs would crack,
And then the shepherd slung him at his back;
And when he rested, to his dog's surprise,
The old fox started from his dead disguise
And while the dog lay panting in the sedge
He up and snapped and bolted through the hedge.

He scampered to the bushes far away:
The shepherd called the ploughman to the fray,
The ploughman wished he had a gun to shoot,
The old dog barked and followed the pursuit,
The shepherd threw his hook and tottered past,
The ploughman ran but none could go so fast,
The woodman threw his faggot from the way
And ceased to chop and wondered at the fray,
But when he saw the dog and heard the cry
He threw his hatchet, but the fox was by –
The shepherd broke his hook and lost the skin –
He found a badger hole and bolted in.
They tried to dig but safe from danger's way
He lived to chase the hounds another day.

The badger grunting on his woodland track
With shaggy hide and sharp nose scrowed with black
Roots in the bushes and the woods and makes
A great huge burrow in the ferns and brakes;

With nose on ground he runs an awk'ard pace
And anything will beat him in the race:
The shepherd's dog will run him to his den
Followed and hooted by the dogs and men;
The woodman when the hunting comes about
Go round at night to stop the foxes out
And hurrying through the bushes, ferns and brakes
Nor sees the many holes the badger makes
And often through the bushes to the chin
Breaks the old holes and tumbles headlong in.

When midnight comes a host of dogs and men
Go out and track the badger to his den
And put a sack within the hole and lie
Till the old grunting badger passes by:
He comes and hears – they let the strongest loose.
The old fox hears the noise and drops the goose;
The poacher shoots and hurries from the cry
And the old hare half-wounded buzzes by.
They get a forkèd stick to bear him down
And clapped the dogs and bore him to the town
And bait him all the day with many dogs
And laugh and shout and fright the scampering hogs –
He runs along and bites at all he meets;
They shout and holler down the noisy streets.

He turns about to face the loud uproar
And drives the rebels to their very doors –
The frequent stone is hurled where'er they go.
When badgers fight and everyone's a foe,
The dogs are clapped and urged to join the fray,
The badger turns and drives them all away;
Though scarcely half as big, dimute and small,
He fights with dogs for hours and beats them all:
The heavy mastiff, savage in the fray,
Lies down and licks his feet and turns away;
The bulldog knows his match and waxes cold,

The badger grins and never leaves his hold.
He drives the crowd and follows at their heels
And bites them through – the drunkard swears and reels.

The frighted women takes the boys away,
The blackguard laughs and hurries in the fray.
He tries to reach the woods, a awk'ard race,
But sticks and cudgels quickly stop the chase.
He turns again and drives the noisy crowd
And beats the many dogs in noises loud;
He drives away and beats them every one
And then they loose them all and set them on.
He falls as dead and kicked by boys and men,
Then starts and grins and drives the crowd again,
Till kicked and torn and beaten out he lies
And leaves his hold and cackles, groans and dies.

[The Vixen]

Among the taller wood with ivy hung
The old fox plays and dances round her young.
She snuffs and barks if any passes by
And swings her tail and turns prepared to fly.
The horseman hurrys by: she bolts to see
And turns again, from danger never free.
If any stands she runs among the poles
And barks and snaps and drives them in the holes.
The shepherd sees them and the boy goes by
And gets a stick and progs the hole to try:
They get all still and lie in safety sure
And out again when safety is secure
And start and snap at blackbirds bouncing by
To fight and catch the great white butterfly.

[Field-Mouse's Nest]

I found a ball of grass among the hay
And progged it as I passed and went away
And when I looked I fancied something stirred
And turned again and hoped to catch the bird,
When out an old mouse bolted in the wheat
With all her young ones hanging at her teats.
She looked so odd and so grotesque to me,
I ran and wondered what the thing could be
And pushed the knapweed bunches where I stood.
When the mouse hurried from the crawling brood
The young ones squeaked, and when I went away
She found her nest again among the hay.
The water o'er the pebbles scarce could run
And broad old sexpools glittered in the sun.

[Wild Bees' Nest]

The mower tramples on the wild bees' nest
And hears the busy noise and stops the rest
Who careless proggle out the mossy ball
And gather up the honey, comb and all.
The boy that seeks dewberries from the sedge
And lays the poison berries on the hedge
Will often find them in the meadow hay
And take his bough and drive the bees away,
But when the maiden goes to turn the hay
She whips her apron up and runs away.
The schoolboy eats the honey, comb and all,
And often knocks his hat against the wall
And progs a stick in every hole he sees
To steal the honey bag of black-nosed bees.

[Autumn Birds]

The wild duck startles like a sudden thought
And heron slow as if it might be caught.
The flopping crows on weary wing go by
And grey beard jackdaws noising as they fly.
The crowds of starnels wiz and hurry by
And darken like a cloud the evening sky.
The larks like thunder rise and suthy round
Then drop and nestle in the stubble ground.
The wild swan hurries high and noises loud
With white necks peering to the evening cloud.
The weary rooks to distant woods are gone;
With length of tail the magpie winnows on
To neighbouring tree and leaves the distant crow
While small birds nestle in the hedge below.

[Stone Pit]

The passing traveller with wonder sees
A deep and ancient stone pit full of trees,
So deep and very deep the place has been
The church might stand within and not be seen.
The passing stranger oft with wonder stops
And thinks he e'en could walk upon their tops
And often stoops to see the busy crow
And stands above and sees the eggs below;
And while the wild horse gives his head a toss
The squirrel dances up and runs across
The boy that stands and kills the black-nosed bee
Dares down as soon as magpies' nests are found
And wonders when he climbs the highest tree
To find it reaches scarce above the ground.

['The old pond full of flags and fenced around']

The old pond full of flags and fenced around
With trees and bushes trailing to the ground;
The water weeds are all around the brink
And one clear place where cattle go to drink
From year to year the schoolboy thither steals
And muddies round the place to catch the eels;
The cowboy, often hiding from the flies,
Lies there and plaits the rushcap as he lies;
The hissing owl sits moping all the day
And hears his song and never flies away;
The pink's nest hangs upon the branch so thin
The young ones caw and seem as tumbling in,
While round them thrums the purple dragonfly
And great white butterfly goes dancing by.

[Trespass]

I dreaded walking where there was no path
And pressed with cautious tread the meadow swath
And always turned to look with wary eye
And always feared the owner coming by;
Yet everything about where I had gone
Appeared so beautiful I ventured on
And when I gained the road where all are free
I fancied every stranger frowned at me
And every kinder look appeared to say
'You've been on trespass in your walk today.'
I've often thought, the day appeared so fine,
How beautiful if such a place were mine;
But, having naught, I never feel alone
And cannot use another's as my own.

Glinton Spire

I love to see the slender spire,
For there the maid of beauty dwells,
And stand again' the hollow tree
And hear the sound of Glinton Bells.

I love to see the boys at play;
The music o'er the summer swells;
I stand among the new-mown hay
And hear the sound of Glinton Bells.

I love the slender spire to see,
For there the maid of beauty dwells,
I think she hears the sound with me
And love to listen Glinton Bells.

And when with songs I used to talk,
I often thought where Mary dwells,
And often took a sabbath walk
And lay and listened Glinton Bells.

I think where Mary's memory stays,
I think where pleasant memory dwells,
I think of happy schoolboy days,
And lie and listen Glinton Bells.

The Gypsy Camp

The snow falls deep, the forest lies alone,
The boy goes hasty for his load of brakes,
Then thinks upon the fire and hurries back;
The gypsy knocks his hands and tucks them up
And seeks his squalid camp half hid in snow
Beneath the oak which breaks away the wind
And bushes close with snow like hovel warm.
There stinking mutton roasts upon the coals
And the half-roasted dog squats close and rubs,
Then feels the heat too strong and goes aloof;
He watches well but none a bit can spare,
And vainly waits the morsel thrown away.
'Tis thus they live – a picture to the place,
A quiet, pilfering, unprotected race.

Graves of Infants

Infants' graves are steps of angels where
Earth's brightest gems of innocence repose;
God is their parent, they need no tear,
He takes them to his bosom from earth's woes,
A bud their life-time and a flower their close.
Their spirits are an iris of the skies,
Needing no prayers – a sunset's happy close.
Gone are the bright rays of their soft blue eyes;
Dews on flowers mourn them, and the gale that sighs.

Their lives were nothing but a sunny shower,
Melting on flowers as tears melt from the eye:
Their death were dew-drops on heaven's amaranthine bower,
'Twas told on flowers as summer gales went by.
They bowed and trembled yet they left no sigh
And the sun smiled to show their end was well.
Infants have nought to weep for ere they die.
All prayers are needless – beads they need not tell;
White flowers their mourners are, nature their passing bell.

Stanzas

Black absence hides upon the past –
  I quite forget thy face
And memory like the angry blast
  Will love's last smile erase.
I try to think of what has been
  But all is blank to me
And other faces pass between
  My early love and thee.

I try to trace thy memory now
  And only find thy name;
Those inky lashes on thy brow,
  Black hair and eyes the same;
Thy round pale face of snowy dyes,
  There's nothing paints thee there;
A darkness comes before my eyes
  For nothing seems so fair.

I knew thy name so sweet and young,
  'Twas music to my ears,
A silent word upon my tongue,
  A hidden thought for years.
Dark hair and lashes swarthy too
  Arched on thy forehead pale –
All else is vanished from my view
  Like voices on the gale.

A Vision

I lost the love of heaven above,
I spurned the lust of earth below,
I felt the sweets of fancied love
And hell itself my only foe.

I lost earth's joys but felt the glow
Of heaven's flame abound in me
Till loveliness and I did grow
The bard of immortality.

I loved but woman fell away
I hid me from her faded fame,
I snatched the sun's eternal ray
And wrote till earth was but a name.

In every language upon earth,
On every shore, o'er every sea,
I gave my name immortal birth
And kept my spirit with the free.

Sonnet

The flag-top quivers in the breeze
That sighs among the willow trees;
In gentle waves the river heaves
That sways like boats the lily-leaves.
The bent-grass trembles as with cold
And crow-flowers nod their cups of gold
Till every dew-drop in them found
Is gently shook upon the ground.
Each wild weed by the river side
In different motions dignified
Bows to the wind, quakes to the breeze,
And charms sweet summer's harmonies.
The very nettle quakes away
To glad the summer's happy day.

The Invitation

Let us go in the fields, love, and see the green tree;
Let's go in the meadows and hear the wild bee;
There's plenty of pleasure for you, love, and me
   In the mirth and the music of nature.
We can stand in the path, love, and hear the birds sing
And see the wood pigeon snap loud on the wing,
While you stand beside me, a beautiful thing,
   Health and beauty in every feature.

We can stand by the brig-foot and see the bright things
On the sun-shining water that merrily springs
Like sparkles of fire in their mazes and rings
   While the insects are glancing, and twitters
You see naught in shape but hear a deep song
That lasts through the sunshine the whole summer long,
That pierces the ear as the heat gathers strong,
   And the lake like a burning fire glitters.

We can stand in the field, love, and gaze o'er the corn,
See the lark from her wing shake the dews of the morn;
Through the dew-beaded woodbine the gale is just born
   And there we can wander, my dearie.
We can walk by the wood where the rabbits pop in,
Where the bushes are few and the hedge gapped and thin;
There's a wild-rosy bower and a place to rest in,
   So we can walk in and rest when we're weary.

The skylark, my love, from the barley is singing,
The hare from her seat of wet clover is springing,
The crow to its nest on the tall elm swinging
   Bears a mouthful of worms for its young.
We'll down the green meadow and up the lone glen
And down the woodside far away from all men,
And there we'll talk over our love-tales again
   Where last year the nightingale sung.

Lines: 'I Am'

I am – yet what I am, none cares or knows;
My friends forsake me like a memory lost:
I am the self-consumer of my woes –
They rise and vanish in oblivion's host
Like shadows in love-frenzied stifled throes –
And yet I am and live – like vapours tossed

Into the nothingness of scorn and noise,
Into the living sea of waking dreams
Where there is neither sense of life or joys
But the vast shipwreck of my life's esteems;
Even the dearest that I love the best
Are strange – nay, rather, stranger than the rest.

I long for scenes where man hath never trod,
A place where woman never smiled or wept,
There to abide with my Creator, God,
And sleep as I in childhood sweetly slept,
Untroubling and untroubled where I lie,
The grass below – above, the vaulted sky.

Sonnet: 'I Am'

I feel I am – I only know I am
And plod upon the earth as dull and void:
Earth's prison chilled my body with its dram
Of dullness and my soaring thoughts destroyed,
I fled to solitudes from passion's dream,
But strife pursued – I only know I am,
I was a being created in the race
Of men disdaining bounds of place and time –
A spirit that could travel o'er the space
Of earth and heaven like a thought sublime,
Tracing creation, like my maker, free –
A soul unshackled – like eternity,
Spurning earth's vain and soul-debasing thrall.
But now I only know I am – that's all.

Song

True love lives in absence,
Like angels we meet her
Dear as dreams of our childhood,
Ay, dearer and sweeter.

The words we remember
By absence unbroken
Are sweeter and dearer
Than when they were spoken.

There's a charm in the eye,
There's a smile on the face
Time, distance or trouble
Can never deface.

The pleasures of childhood
Were angels above
And the hopes of my manhood
All centred in love.

The scenes where we met,
Ay, the joys of our childhood,
There's nothing so sweet
As those fields of the wildwood

Where we met in the morning,
The noon and the gloaming
And stayed till the moon
High in heaven was roaming.

Friends meet and are happy,
So are hopes fixed above;
But there's nothing so dear
As first meetings of love.

Autumn

The thistledown's flying though the winds are all still
On the green grass now lying, now mounting the hill.
The spring from the fountain now boils like a pot.
Through stones past the counting it bubbles red-hot.

The ground parched and cracked is like overbaked bread,
The greensward all wrecked is bents dried up and dead.
The fallow fields glitter like water indeed
And gossamers twitter flung from weed unto weed.

Hill-tops like hot iron glitter hot i' the sun
And the rivers we're eyeing burn to gold as they run.
Burning hot is the ground, liquid gold is the air:
Whoever looks round sees eternity there.

Sonnet: Wood Anemone

The wood anemone through dead oak leaves
And in the thickest woods now blooms anew,
And where the green briar and the bramble weaves
Thick clumps o'green, anemones thicker grew,
And weeping flowers in thousands pearled in dew
People the woods and brakes, hid hollows there,
White, yellow and purple-hued the wide wood through.
What pretty drooping weeping flowers they are:
The clipt-frilled leaves, the slender stalk they bear
On which the drooping flower hangs weeping dew.
How beautiful through April time and May
The woods look, filled with wild anemone;
And every little spinney now looks gay
With flowers mid brushwood and the huge oak tree.

Sonnet: The Crow

How peaceable it seems for lonely men
To see a crow fly in the thin blue line
Over the woods and fields, o'er level fen:
It speaks of villages or cottage nigh
Behind the neighbouring woods. When March winds high
Tear off the branches of the huge old oak,
I love to see these chimney sweeps sail by
And hear them o'er the gnarlèd forest croak,
Then sosh askew from the hid woodman's stroke
That in the woods their daily labours ply.
I love the sooty crew nor would provoke
Its March day exercise of croaking joy;
I love to see it sailing to and fro
While fields and woods and waters spread below.

Clock-a-clay

In the cowslip's peeps I lie
Hidden from the buzzing fly
While green grass beneath me lies
Pearled wi' dew like fishes' eyes.
Here I lie, a clock-a-clay,
Waiting for the time o'day.

While grassy forests quake surprise
And the wild wind sobs and sighs,
My gold home rocks as like to fall
On its pillars green and tall;
When the pattering rain drives by
Clock-a-clay keeps warm and dry.

Day by day and night by night
All the week I hide from sight;
In the cowslip's peeps I lie,
In rain and dew still warm and dry;
Day and night and night and day
Red black-spotted clock-a-clay.

My home it shakes in wind and showers,
Pale green pillar topped wi' flowers,
Bending at the wild wind's breath
Till I touch the grass beneath.
Here still I live, lone clock-a-clay,
Watching for the time of day.

[The Thunder Mutters]

The thunder mutters louder and more loud;
With quicker motion hay folks ply the rake;
Ready to burst, slow sails the pitch black cloud
And all the gang a bigger haycock make
To sit beneath – the woodland winds awake
The drops so large. Wet all thro' in an hour
A tiny flood runs down the leaning rake
In the sweet hay, yet dry the hay folks cower,
And some beneath the waggon shun the shower.

The Yellowhammer

When shall I see the whitethorn leaves again,
And yellowhammers gath'ring the dry bents
By the dyke-side on stilly moor or fen,
Feathered wi'love and nature's good intents?
Rude is the nest this architect invents,
Rural the place, wi' cart-ruts by dyke-side;
Dead grass, horse hair and downy-headed bents
Tied to dead thistles she doth well provide,
Close to a hill o'ants where cowslips bloom
And shed o'er meadows far their sweet perfume.
In early spring when winds blow chilly cold
The yellowhammer trailing grass will come
To fix a place and choose an early home
With yellow breast and head of solid gold.

To John Clare

Well, honest John, how fare you now at home?
The spring is come and birds are building nests,
The old cock robin to the sty is come
With olive feathers and its ruddy breast,
And the old cock with wattles and red comb
Struts with the hens and seems to like some best,
Then crows and looks about for little crumbs
Swept out by little folks an hour ago;
The pigs sleep in the sty, the book man comes,
The little boys lets home-close nesting go
And pockets tops and taws where daisies bloom
To look at the new number just laid down
With lots of pictures and good stories too
And Jack-the-giant-killer's high renown.

Birds' Nests

The very child might understand
The De'il had business on his hand – Robert Burns

'Tis spring, warm glows the south,
Chaffinches carry the moss in his mouth
To the filbert hedges all day long
And charms the poet with his beautiful song
– The wind blows blea o'er the sedgy fen,
But warm the sun shines by the little wood
Where the old cow at her leisure chews her cud.

Glossary

'awe	haws, hawthorne fruit
bawk	strip of grass dividing ploughed fields (also: bauk or baulk)
bee-spell	the spotted patterning in a glass marble
besom	sweeper
blackcap	the migrant warbler, *Sylvia atricapilla* (Clare's sonnet collected here, 'The Blackcap', is actually the great tit, *Parus major*).
blea	bleak, raw, exposed
blood-walls	wild wallflowers
brake	thickets of bramble or fern
brig	bridge
bumbarrel	the long-tailed tit, *Aegithalos caudatus*
'cat gallows sticks'	two sticks stuck vertically in the ground, with a third across them, used for jumping games
chock	pitching marbles
clack	chatter
'clink and bandy'	game in which a piece of wood is sprung then struck using a stick
clock-a-clay	ladybird
closen	small enclosures, fields; the Saxon plural
clout	to clothe; to patch or repair
clown	a rustic
clumpsing	numb with cold
crankle	to bend or twist
crizzled	just beginning to freeze over; filmy ice
cuckoo flower	early purple orchid
dewberry	similar to blackberry, *Rubus caesius*
dotterel	pollarded tree

ducking stone	game using a mounted stone which other stones are thrown at
edding	grass at the head of a field
elting	soft ridges of freshly ploughed land
fern owl	the nightjar, *Caprimulgus europaeus*
flags	rushes and reeds
flaze	flaring candle flame, as in moving air
frit	frightened
furmety	baked wheat and milk drink, sweetened with sugar and plums, thickened with flour and eggs
gelid	jelly-like
glib	smooth and slippery
grubbing gear	digging equipment
heathbell	flower of the heath
henbane	narcotic plant, *Hyoscyamus niger*
hing	hang
horse-blob	marsh marigold, *Caltha palustris*
king cup	marsh marigold, *Caltha palustris*
ladycow	ladybird
lady-smocks	cuckoo-flower, *Cardamine pratensis*
land rail	the corncrake, *Crex crex*
ling	heather, *Calluna vulgaris*
lown	man of low birth
maul	toil along, drag wearily (also: moil)
mavis	the song thrush, *Turdus philomelos*
mort	a great amount
mouldywarps	moles
oddling	odd-one-out
old-mans-beard	*Clematis vitalba*
peep	single blossom of flower growing in a cluster
pink	the chaffinch, *Fringilla coelebs* (and sometimes the yellowhammer, *Emberiza citrinella*)
pismire	ant

pleachy	mellow, powdery
prog, progged	to poke about: proggling-stick
puddock	the kite or buzzard
ramping	to grow in abundance, luxuriantly
rank	luxuriantly
rawky	misty or foggy
rout	route; great stir or commotion
sawn	to saunter
scrowed	lined
sexpools	rainwater pools in peat workings
soodling	to saunter lazily; to dawdle
sosh	plunge or dip
spindle	shoot up
sprent	sprinkled
starnels	the starling, *Sturnus vulgaris*
startling	startled
stulp	tree-stump
sturt	start suddenly
suthy	a sighing or rushing noise
swaily	shady
swaths	row of scythed hay, left to dry
swee	swing or sway
swop/swopping	swoop/swooping
taw	marble
teasel	prickly-headed plant, *Dipsacus fullonum*
tenting	watching, attending
younkers	youngsters